KnitWit

KnitWit

20 Fun Projects for Beginners and Seasoned Knitters

KATIE BOYETTE

SELLERS

PUBLISHING

Published by **Sellers Publishing, Inc.**
161 John Roberts Road, Portland, Maine 04106

Visit our Web Site: www.sellerspublishing.com
E-mail: rsp@rsvp.com

Design and layout copyright © BlueRed Press Ltd 2010
Text copyright © Katie Boyette
Patterns and templates copyright © Katie Boyette
All rights reserved.
Design by Matt Windsor

ISBN 13: 978-1-4162-0608-8
Library of Congress Number 2010921820

10 9 8 7 6 5 4 3 2

Printed and Bound in China

Knitting Needle Sizes

Metric (mm)	U.S.
2.0	0
2.25	1
2.75	2
3.0	-
3.25	3
3.5	4
3.75	5
4.0	6
4.5	7
5.0	8
5.5	9
6.0	10
6.5	10.5
7.0	-
7.5	-
8.0	11
9.0	13
10.0	15
12.75	17
15.0	19
19.0	35
25.0	50

courtesy of the Craft Yarn Council, Gastonia, N.C.

Contents

Introduction

Five years ago, I was a stay-at-home mom, living here in the mountains of North Carolina. I had an art degree that was not being used, and a craving to get out of the house, socialize, and be creative. A friend suggested that I join her local *Stitch and Bitch* group. I had never heard of such a thing, and was intrigued, though truthfully, I had no interest at all in learning to knit. I joined this lively group of women every Wednesday night at a local bar. I brought along my needlework and attended regularly for months, before a member handed me a set of spare needles and strong-armed me into giving knitting a try. I was instantly obsessed.

Three years ago, I knitted my first toy from a pattern in a magazine. I immediately fell in love with the process. Toys knit up quickly, are great projects for using up leftover balls of yarn, and there's never a worry about size and fit. Best of all, I found that knitted toys appeal to people of all ages, and truthfully, there's nothing more fun than taking a new project to your knitting group and watching your friends *ooh* and *ahh* over what you've created.

A while ago I began experimenting with creating my own patterns. At the time, I was collaborating on a gallery show with a friend. As part of the show, I created a monster for each of my friend's children. They were based on a particular bad habit the child had at the time.

Most of the projects in this book are knit in the round. This reduces the amount of time spent seaming, and also makes it easier to stuff the toys as you go. Often when knitting toys, it's hard to imagine the finished piece until the "aha moment" when you fill the fabric with polyester toy stuffing and watch it come to life. The felt embellishments give the toys more character, making their moods and expressions limitless.

I journal my adventures in knitting and toy-making, as well as the life events that inspire them at **www.caffaknitted.typepad.com**.

Katie Boyette

Owls

When I was growing up, the woods surrounding our house were frequented by little screech owls. We could hear their haunting calls at night, but I never saw them. I've loved the sound ever since. A few years ago, my cat captured a nest of sparrow chicks. In a desperate attempt to save them, I took the entire family to a wildlife refuge and rehab center here in the mountains. While touring the center, one of the vets introduced me to a nest of screech owl hatchlings someone had saved. There they were, three incredibly fluffy little balls of gray feathers with enormous sleepy yellow eyes. I was immediately smitten.

Materials

For small owl:
- 1 skein Cascade 220 in 8907
- 1 skein Cascade 220 in 8010 for feet
- 1 set US 5 (3.75mm) double pointed needles

For large owl:
- 1 skein Cascade Jewel 9931
- 1 skein Cascade Jewel 9890 for feet
- 1 set US 8 (5mm) double pointed needles
- 2 safety pins
- Toy stuffing
- Scraps of wool felt for eyes and beaks in black, white, beige and orange
- Embroidery needle
- Straight pins

Glossary of abbreviations

CO	cast on
dpn	double pointed needles(s)
k	knit
k2tog	knit two together
kfb	knit into front and back of stitch
pm	place marker
st[s]	stitch[es]

Body (Knit from the top down)
For the large owl, knit the entire owl on size 8 needles. For the small owl knit the entire pattern on size 5 needles.
CO 5, pm and join to knit in the round.
Round 1: Kfb 5 times. 10 sts
Round 2: (kfb, k1) 5 times. 15 sts
Round 3: (kfb, k2) 5 times. 20 sts
Round 4: (kfb, k3) 5 times. 25 sts
Knit 7 rows even. Place all stitches on a piece of contrasting scrap yarn. Repeat rows 1–11 again, to make second eye.

Place first 6 stitches from each eye on a needle. Place the eyes side by side, needles parallel, upside-down like two little cups…or a little bra. Reattach yarn. Take the first stitch from each needle and knit together. Continue to knit together each consecutive stitch. After you finish

the row, and have 6 stitches, turn and knit back across the row, binding off as you go. When you have one stitch remaining, carefully pick up the next stitch to the left from the contrasting yarn. Be sure to bind off remaining stitch from the center of the eyes. Pick up and knit each remaining stitch around the perimeter of the owl, distributing them evenly among the needles. When you complete the row, pm, and knit another row in the round. 38 sts.
Round 3: K7, kfb, k3, kfb, k14, kfb, k3, kfb, k7. 42 sts.
Round 4: Knit.
Round 5: K7, kfb, k5, kfb, k14, kfb, k5, kfb, k7. 46 sts.
Round 6: Knit.
Round 7: K7, kfb, k7, kfb, k14, kfb, k7, kfb, k7. 50 sts

For large owl: knit 15 rounds even.
For small owl: knit 10 rounds even.

Decreasing the bottom
Round 1: (K2tog, k8) 5 times. 45 sts
Round 2: (K2tog, k7) 5 times. 40 sts
Round 3: (K2tog, k6) 5 times. 35 sts
Round 4: (K2tog, k5) 5 times. 30 sts
Round 5: (K2tog, k4) 5 times. 25 sts
Round 6: (K2tog, k3) 5 times. 20 sts
Pause at this point to stuff the toy, poking and squeezing the eyes to get the desired shape.

Round 7: (K2tog, k2) 5 times. 15 sts
Round 8: (K2tog, k1) 5 times. 10 sts
Round 9: K2tog all the way around. 5 sts
Fill the toy to the top. Cut yarn and pull through remaining stitches, pull tight, knot, and use yarn needle to pull knot to

inside of toy.

Feet

In contrasting color, CO 4. Divide stitches between 2 dpn needles. Join in the round.

Knit 10 rounds.

Next round: Kfb 4 times. 8 sts

Next round: Kfb, k2, kfb 2 twice, k2, kfb. 12 sts

At this point you will divide the stitches to knit the toes. Put the first 4 stitches from the top needle on a safety pin, and the 4 stitches below on the other needle on another safety pin.

Right toe

Knit the remaining 2 stitches from the top needle, turn, and knit the 2 remaining stitches from the bottom needle. Join to knit in the round. Knit 7 rounds. K2tog twice. Cut yarn.

Leave 6 inch tail. Pull yarn through 2 remaining stitches and knot. Using a yarn needle, run tail downward through the stitches along the bottom of the toe. Pull until toe has the desired curve. Knot, and pull into toe.

Middle toe

Pick up the middle two stitches from the top and bottom needles. Follow the directions for the first toe.

Left toe

Follow directions for first toe with the remaining 4 stitches.

Wings (make 2)

Knit the first and last stitch of every row.

CO 5

Row 1: Knit.

Row 2: K1, p3, K1.

Row 3: K1, kfb, k1, kfb, k1. 7 sts

Row 4: K1, p5, k1.

Row 5: Knit.

Row 6: K1, p5, k1.

Row 7: K1, kfb, k3, kfb, k1. 9 sts

Continue to increase 2 stitches every fourth row until you have 13 sts. Knit 2 rows even.

Bind off.

Assembly

Feet

Place the feet in the shape of a V, and sit the body on top. Adjust the position of the feet until they look symmetrical. Use straight pins to secure them in place on the bottom of the owl. Use a yarn needle and the long tail from the foot, sew into the body, parallel to the foot, then through the foot, and down through the body along the other side. Continue this until the foot has been secured to the base of the claw. Repeat for other foot.

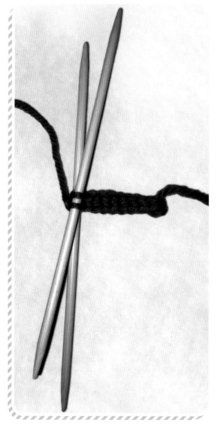

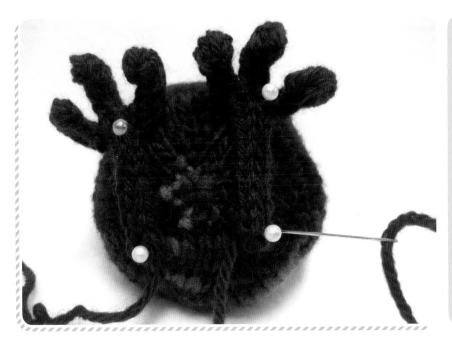

Wings
The placement of the wings is optional. They can be secured to the sides flat all the way down, or can be folded in half, to the shape of a triangle, and attached along the side of the body.

Face
From scraps of felt, cut 2 each of: Eyeballs in white, iris, pupils in black, eyelids in beige.
Cut one triangle from orange felt for beak.
Cut embroidery floss and using a blanket stitch to attach eyes to head, doing one circle at a time.
For the beak, use a matching color of thread and a ladder stitch to attach between eyes.

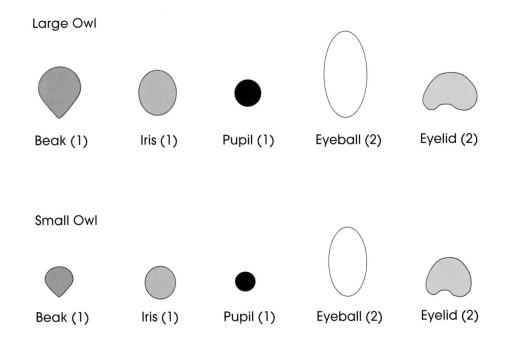

Large Owl

Beak (1)   Iris (1)   Pupil (1)   Eyeball (2)   Eyelid (2)

Small Owl

Beak (1)   Iris (1)   Pupil (1)   Eyeball (2)   Eyelid (2)

Frank

Just because a monster is very small, that doesn't mean he can't be stylish. I'm quite fond of making tiny hats from felt. Frank definitely needed one the most, to keep the sun out of his one big eye. From the smile on his face, you can see that he's very happy with his appearance.

Materials

- 1 skein Cascade 220 in 7816
- 1 set US 6 (4mm) double pointed needles
- Scraps of wool felt in white, black and dark blue
- Toy stuffing
- Yarn needle
- Embroidery needle
- Thread
- Black embroidery floss

Glossary of abbreviations

CO	cast on
dpn	double pointed needles(s)
k	knit
k2tog	knit two together
kfb	knit into front and back of stitch
pm	place marker
st[s]	stitch[es]

Body

Using US 6 (4mm) dpn, CO 6, pm, join to knit in the round. Split stitches evenly between 3 needles.
Round 1: Kfb 6 times. 12 sts
Round 2 and all even numbered rounds: Knit.
Round 3: (Kfb, k1) 6 times. 18 sts
Round 5: (Kfb, k2) 6 times. 24 sts
Round 7: (Kfb, k3) 6 times. 30 sts
Round 9: (Kfb, k4) 6 times. 36 sts
Rounds 10–21: Knit.
Round 22: (K2tog, k4) 6 times. 30 sts
Rounds 23–24: Knit.
Round 25: (K2tog, k3) 6 times. 24 sts
Pause and stuff body nearly full.
Rounds 26–27: Knit.
Continue to decrease 6 sts every third round until 3 sts remain.
Break yarn. Pull tail through remaining stitches. Fill rest of body with stuffing. Pull tight, knot and pull tail to inside of toy.

Legs (make 2)

CO 5, pm, join to knit in the round.
Round 1: Kfb 5 times. 10 sts
Round 2: (Kfb, k1) 5 times. 15 sts
Round 3: (Kfb, k2) 5 times. 20 sts
Knit 4 rounds even. Bind off.

Arms (make 2)

CO 5, pm, join to knit in the round.
Round 1: Kfb 5 times. 10 sts
Round 2: (Kfb, k1) 5 times. 15 sts
Knit 6 rounds even. Bind off.

Assembly

Center legs on lower front of body, spacing ½ in. apart. Begin attaching using scrap of blue yarn and a ladder stitch. Once the seam is 2/3 complete, stuff leg full. Finish seaming, knot, and pull knot to inside of toy.
Repeat for second leg. For the arms, press flat, and attach to sides of body using mattress stitch.
Cut felt pieces using templates.

Eye

Center eyeball on the front of the body. Use a single strand of black embroidery floss and embroidery needle to attach to face. Follow in the same manner with pupil. Using a thick strand of black embroidery floss, sew a line for the smile under the eye.

Hat

Wrap side of hat around the top, using straight pins to hold in place, overlapping slightly on the sides. Sew into place using single strand of sewing thread. Place brim on hat on a flat surface. Center top of hat on brim. Sew around the edge, securing brim to hat, placing stitches evenly every 1/8 inch. Secure with a knot.

EYE EYE! KNIT ME A MONOCLE!

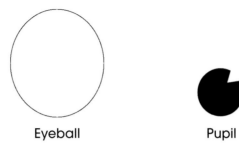

Eyeball

Pupil

Side of hat

Brim of hat

Top of hat

Otto

One of my favorite pastimes is bird watching. My daughter and I spend a great deal of time on our porch while I knit, watching the various birds come to our feeder. Sophia fancies herself quite the ornithologist, imitating bird calls, drawing pictures, and discussing the different breeds. When she isn't sure what type of bird has come for a visit, she generally makes up a name for it. She has pages upon pages of her own imaginary guide to birds. Otto was inspired by one of these imaginary breeds.

Materials

- 1 skein Cascade 220 in 9427
- 1 skein Cascade 220 in 7822
- 1 set US 6 (4mm) double pointed needles
- Scraps of wool felt in white, black and light blue
- Toy stuffing
- Yarn needle
- Embroidery needle
- Thread
- 2 safety pins

Glossary of abbreviations

CO	cast on
dpn	double pointed needles(s)
k	knit
k2tog	knit two together
kfb	knit into front and back of stitch
p	purl
pm	place marker
st[s]	stitch[es]
St st	stockinette stitch

Body

Using US 6 (4mm) dpn, CO 6, pm join to knit in the round. Split stitches evenly between 3 needles.

Round 1: Kfb 6 times. 12 sts
Round 2 and all even numbered rounds: Knit.
Round 3: (Kfb, k1) 6 times. 18 sts
Round 5: (Kfb, k2) 6 times. 24 sts
Round 7: (Kfb, k3) 6 times. 30 sts
Round 9: (Kfb, k4) 6 times. 36 sts
Round 11: (Kfb, k5) 6 times. 42 sts
Round 13: (Kfb, k6) 6 times. 48 sts
Round 15: (Kfb, k7) 6 times. 54 sts
Knit 22 rounds even.
Round 37: (K2tog, k7) 6 times. 48 sts
Round 39: (K2tog, k6) 6 times. 42 sts
Round 41: (K2tog, k5) 6 times. 36 sts
Round 43: (K2tog, k4) 6 times. 30 sts
Round 45: (K2tog, k3) 6 times. 24 sts
Pause and stuff body nearly full.
Round 47: (K2tog, k2) 6 times. 18 sts
Round 49: (K2tog, k1) 6 times. 12 sts
Round 51: K2tog 6 times. 6 sts
Break yarn. Pull tail through remaining stitches. Fill rest of body with stuffing.

Pull tight, knot and pull tail to inside of toy.

Wings

Right wing

Using US 6 needles, CO 7.
Row 1: Kfb, k5, kfb. 9 sts
Row 2: Purl.
Row 3: Kfb, k7, kfb. 11 sts
Row 4: Purl.
Row 5: K2tog, k9. 10 sts
Row 6: Purl.
Continue in stockinette stitch, decreasing one stitch at the beginning of each knit row, until 1 stitch remains. Pull tail through last stitch, and weave tail into purl side of wing.

Left wing

Complete rows 1–4 as for right wing.
Row 5: K9, k2tog. 10 sts
Row 6: Purl.
Continue in stockinette stitch, decreasing one stitch at the end of each knit row until one stitch remains. Finish same as for right wing.

Legs

Using brown yarn, CO 3.
Knit an i-cord 2 in. long.
(Making an i-cord: Knit, don't turn. Slip the sts back to the beginning of the needle and k the row again. Continue in this manner until you have knitted 2 in. Pull down on the cord and the gap at the back will close.)
Next round: Kfb, k1, kfb. 5 sts
Continue pulling yarn across back of stitches as an i-cord.
Next round: K1, kfb, k1, kfb, k1. 7 sts
Knit 2 rounds.
Next round: K1, k2tog, k1, k2tog, k1. 5 sts
Next round: K2tog, k1, k2tog. 3 sts
Knit 3 in. of i-cord.
Next round: Kfb, k1, kfb. 5 sts
Next round: K2, kfb, k2. 6 sts
Next round: Kfb, k4, kfb. 8 sts
Split stitches between 2 needles. Knit in the round.
Next round: Kfb, k2, kfb twice, k2, kfb.

12 sts
Next round: Kfb, k4, kfb twice, k4, kfb.
16 sts
Next round: K3, kfb, k6, kfb, k3. 18 sts

At this point you will divide the stitches to knit the toes. Put the first 6 stitches from the top needle on a safety pin, and the 6 stitches below on the other needle on another safety pin.

Right toe
Knit the remaining 3 stitches from the top needle, turn, and knit the 3 remaining stitches from the bottom needle. Join to knit in the round.
Knit 7 rows. K2tog 3 times. Cut yarn. Leave 6 in tail. Pull yarn through remaining stitches and knot. Using a yarn needle, run tail downward through the stitches along the bottom of the toe. Pull until toe has the desired curve. Knot, and pull into toe.

Middle toe
Pick up the middle three stitches from the top and bottom needles. Follow the directions for the first toe.

Left toe
Follow directions for first toe with the remaining 6 stitches.

Top feathers:
Using brown yarn, CO 2. Knit 3 i-cords in the following lengths: ½ in., 1 in., 1 ½ in.

Assembly

Attach wings to side of body using ladder stitch.
Sew legs to bottom of body, securing firmly.
Cut small blue feathers from felt and attach to the i-cords using image as reference. Attach to top of head.
Cut pieces of felt using the templates. Sew eyeballs, and then pupils using black thread and a mattress stitch. Sew belly onto body using the same thread and mattress stitch.

Feathers (3)

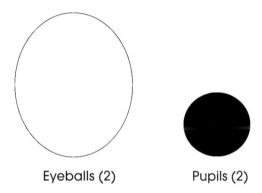

Eyeballs (2)   Pupils (2)

Belly

Flop

Flop is one of my earliest monsters. He earned his name while participating in an art show. Sitting on a shelf in the gallery, he had the terrible habit of flopping over onto his side every time someone walked past. After some quick corrective surgery on his foot placement, Flop finally managed to sit upright and stable, but his affectionate nickname remained. When Jamie, a fellow studio-mate, agreed to trade her photography skills in return for a piece of my work, she eagerly chose to take him home with her.

Materials

- 1 skein Cascade 220 in 7818 (blue)
- 1 skein Cascade 220 in 9476 (yellow)
- 1 skein Cascade 128 chunky in 7802 (fuchsia)
- 1 set US 7 (4.5mm) double pointed needles
- 1 set US 9 (5.5mm) double pointed needles
- Scraps of felt in white, pink, and black
- Pink thread
- Toy stuffing
- Yarn needle
- Embroidery needle
- 2 safety pins

Glossary of abbreviations

CO	cast on
dpn	double pointed needles
k	knit
k2tog	knit two together
kfb	knit into front and back of stitch
p	purl
pfb	purl into front and back of stitch
pm	place marker
ssk	slip, slip, knit slipped stitches together
st[s]	stitch[es]

Body

Using US 9 (5.5mm) dpn needles and fuchsia yarn CO 6, pm join to knit in the round. Split stitches evenly between 3 needles.

Round 1: Kfb 6 times. 12 sts

Round 2 and all even numbered rounds: Knit.

Round 3: (Kfb, k1) 6 times. 18 sts

Round 5: (Kfb, k2) 6 times. 24 sts

Round 7: (Kfb, k3) 6 times. 30 sts

Round 9: (Kfb, k4) 6 times. 36 sts

Round 11: (Kfb, k5) 6 times. 42 sts

Round 13: (Kfb, k6) 6 times. 48 sts

Round 15: (Kfb, k7) 6 times. 54 sts

Rounds 16–18: Knit.

Switch to US 7 (4.5mm) needles and blue yarn.

Round 19: K8, k2tog, k7, ssk, k16, k2tog, k7, ssk, k8. 50 sts

Rounds 20–23: Knit.

Round 24: K7, k2tog, k7, ssk, k14, k2tog, k7, ssk, k7. 46 sts

Switch back to US 9 (5.5mm) needles and fuchsia yarn.

Rounds 25–26: Knit.

Round 27: K6, k2tog, k7, ssk, k12, k2tog, k7, ssk, k6. 42 sts

Round 28: Knit.

Round 29: K5, k2tog, k7, ssk, k10, k2tog, k7, ssk, k5. 38 sts

Round 30: Knit.

Switch back to US 7 (4.5mm) needles and blue yarn.

Knit 25 rounds even.

Divide for eyes.

Round 1: K7 on one dpn needle, k5 on the second dpn needle, k7 on a third needle, CO 5 to the fourth needle. Put the remaining 19 sts on a piece of scrap yarn. Pm, and join to knit in the round.

Rounds 2–3: Knit.

Round 4: (Kfb, k5, kfb twice, k3, kfb) twice. 32 sts

Round 5: Knit.

Round 6: (Kfb, k7, kfb twice, k5, kfb) twice. 40 sts

Rounds 7–10: Knit.

Round 11: (K2tog, k7, ssk, k2tog, k5, ssk) twice. 32 sts

Round 12: Knit.

Round 13: (K2tog, k5, ssk, k2tog, k3, ssk) twice. 24 sts

Round 14: Knit.

Round 15: (K2tog, k2) 6 times. 18 sts

Round 16: Knit.

Round 17: (K2tog, k1) 6 times. 12 sts

Round 18: Knit.

Round 19: K2tog 6 times. 6 sts

Break yarn, pull tail through remaining sts, knot, and pull to inside of toy.

Stuff body and finished eye firmly.

Reattach yarn. Pick up and knit sts from scrap yarn in the same manner as for first eye. CO 5, pm, join to knit in the round. Complete the same as for first eye. Stuff firmly before closing up stitches.

Lip

Using blue yarn and US 7 (4.5) needles, CO 12.

Rows 1–3: Stockinette st.
Row 4: P1, pfb, p8, pfb, p1. 14 sts
Row 5: Knit.
Row 6: P4, pfb, p4, pfb, p4. 16 sts
Row 7: Knit.
Row 8: P5, pfb, p4, pfb, p5. 18 sts
Row 9: Knit.
Row 10: P6, pfb, p4, pfb, p6. 20 sts
Row 11: Knit.
Bind off.

Feet (knit 2)

Using yellow yarn and US 7 (4.5)

needles, CO 6. Divide stitches between 2 dpn needles. Join to knit in the round. Knit 12 rounds.
Next round: (Kfb, k1, kfb) twice. 10 sts
Next round: Knit.
Next round: (Kfb, k3, kfb) twice. 14 sts
Next round: Knit.
Next round: (Kfb, k5, kfb) twice. 18 sts

At this point you will divide the stitches to knit the toes. Put the first 6 stitches from the top needle on a safety pin, and the 6 stitches below on the other needle on another safety pin.

Right toe

Knit the remaining 3 stitches from the top needle, turn, and knit the 3 remaining

stitches from the bottom needle. Join to knit in the round. Knit 7 rows. Cut yarn. Leave 6 in. tail. Pull yarn through 6 remaining stitches and knot. Using a yarn needle, run tail downward through the stitches along the bottom of the toe. Pull until toe has the desired curve. Knot, and pull into toe.

Middle toe

Pick up the middle 3 stitches from the top and bottom needles. Follow the directions for the first toe.

Left toe

Stuff foot lightly. Follow directions for first toe with the remaining 6 stitches.

Assembly

Cut all pieces from felt using template. Center teeth on face and attach using pink thread and blanket stitch. Center eyes on face and sew into place using pink thread, beginning with white, followed by pink, and then black. Center lip over teeth. Use the tail to sew around the perimeter of the bottom, allowing the bound off edge to curl down revealing teeth. Center feet on bottom of body. Use the tail from the cast on edge to sew feet into place.

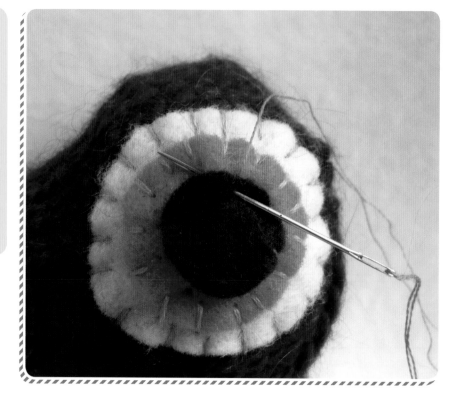

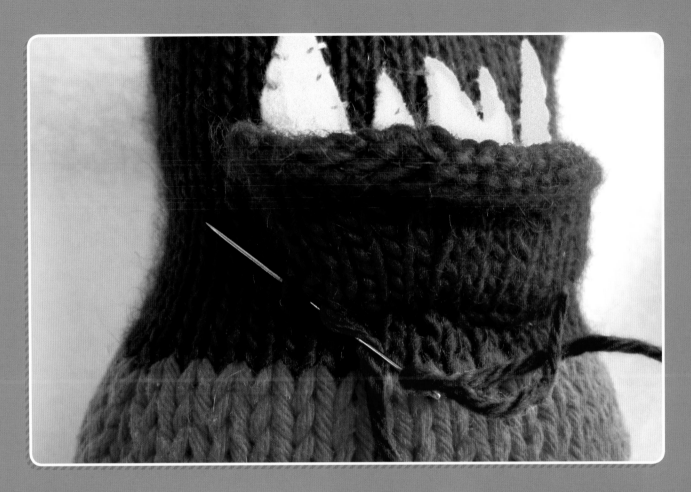

Eye (2)

Iris (2)

Pupil (2)

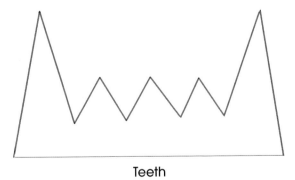

Teeth

Dave

Dave is the funniest monster I know. He's fond of telling jokes, and does the best escalator impression you've ever seen. He often speaks in a fake Russian accent, and leaves absurd messages on my voicemail. He's also frequently late for work, and some days he's too lazy to even put on his pants, but somehow that just makes him that much more loveable.

Materials

- 1 skein Cascade 220 in 9443
- Small amount of white yarn
- 1 set US 6 (4mm) double pointed needles
- Scraps of wool felt in white and black
- Toy stuffing
- Yarn needle
- Embroidery needle
- Thread

Glossary of abbreviations

CO	cast on
k	knit
k2tog	knit two together
kfb	knit into front and back of stitch
pm	place marker
st[s]	stitch[es]

Legs (make 2)
CO 6, pm, join to knit in the round.
Round 1: Kfb 6 times. 12 sts
Round 2 and all even rounds: Knit.
Round 3: (Kfb, k1) 6 times. 18 sts
Round 4: (Kfb, k2) 6 times. 24 sts
Rounds 5–14: Knit.
Place all stitches on a piece of contrasting scrap yarn.

Connect legs and begin body
Place first 6 stitches from each leg on a needle. Place the legs side by side, needles parallel, upside-down like two little cups...or a little bra. Reattach yarn. Take the first stitch from each needle and knit together.

Continue to knit together each consecutive stitch. After you finish the row, and have 6 stitches, turn and knit back across the row, binding off as you go.

When you have one stitch remaining, carefully pick up the next stitch to the left from the contrasting yarn. Be sure to bind off remaining stitch from the center of the legs.

Pick up and knit each remaining stitch around the perimeter of the legs, distributing them evenly among the needles.
When you complete the row, pm, and knit another row in the round.

Continue body
Rounds 1–4: Knit. 36 sts
Round 5: K13, kfb, k8, kfb, k13. 38 sts
Round 6 and all even numbered rounds: Knit.
Round 7: K13, kfb, k10, kfb, k13. 40 sts
Round 9: K13, kfb, k12, kfb, k13. 42 sts
Round 11: K13, kfb, k14, kfb, k13. 44 sts
Rounds 12–14: Knit.
Round 15: K13, k2tog, k14, k2tog, k13. 42 sts
Round 17: K13, k2tog, k12, k2tog, k13. 40 sts
Round 19: K13, k2tog, k10, k2tog, k13. 38 sts
Round 21: K13, k2tog, k8, k2tog, k13. 36 sts
Rounds 22–31: Knit.
Stuff toy almost full.
Round 32: (K2tog, k4) 6 times. 30 sts
Round 33 and all odd numbered rounds: Knit.
Round 34: (K2tog, k3) 6 times. 24 sts
Continue to decrease 6 sts every other round until 6 sts remain. Fill toy completely with stuffing. Break yarn, pull tail through remaining sts, knot, and pull knot to inside of toy.

Arms (make 2)
CO 6, pm, join to knit in the rounds.
Round 1: Kfb 6 times. 12 sts
Rounds 2–4: Knit.
Round 5: K2tog, k4, k2tog twice, k4, k2tog. 8 sts
Rounds 6–14: Knit.
Bind off.

Big eye
Using white yarn, CO 6, pm, join to knit in the round.
Round 1: Kfb 6 times. 12 sts
Round 2: (Kfb, k1) 6 times. 18 sts
Round 3: (Kfb, k2) 6 times. 24 sts
Rounds 4–8: Knit.
Bind off.

Little eye
Using white yarn, CO 6, pm, join to knit
in the round.
Round 1: Kfb 6 times. 12 sts
Round 2: (Kfb, k1) 6 times. 18 sts
Rounds 3–7: Knit.
Bind off.

Assembly

Fold arms flat, use mattress stitch to
attach to sides of body. Center eyes
on front of face, using straight pins to
secure. Sew around the perimeter using
mattress stitch, pausing when eye is 2/3
attached to stuff with filling.

Cut all felt pieces from template. Attach
pupils to eyes using black thread and
blanket stitch. Attach briefs using white
thread and blanket stitch. Using 3
strands of dark gray embroidery floss,
and a straight stitch, follow lines on
template to create detail on briefs.
Attach mouth, beginning with black
center, and sewing the lips over it.

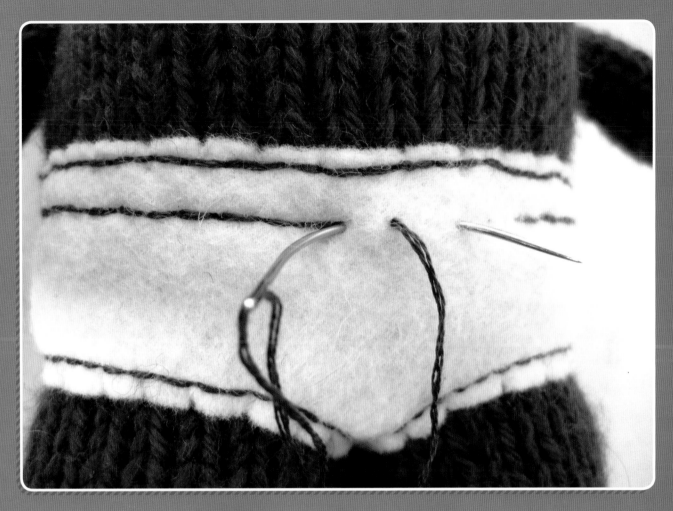

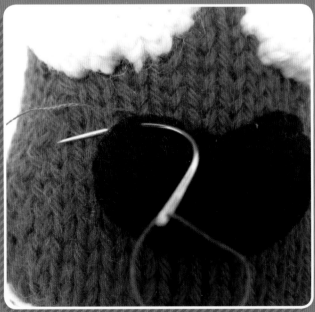

Pupils

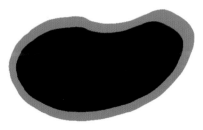

Mouth

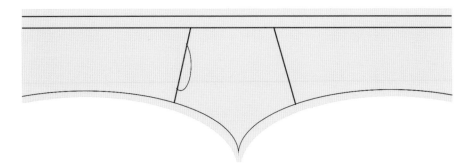

Briefs (2)

Bo Peeps

I really love Cascade's chunky baby alpaca. It is the perfect yarn for a super soft baby toy. I felt it was the best choice for a rather floppy, and slightly excessively happy, bunny. My daughter agreed, as this quickly became her favorite toy of all the ones I've knitted. The alpaca is so soft, and the bunny is the perfect size for being lugged around. This bunny has seen a lot of love.

Materials

- 1 skein Cascade Baby Alpaca Chunky in 562 (teal)
- 1 skein Cascade Baby Alpaca Chunky in 559 (light blue)
- 1 set US 7 (4.5mm) double pointed needles
- Scraps of wool felt in white, black and light blue
- Toy stuffing
- Yarn needle
- Embroidery needle
- Thread

Glossary of abbreviations

CO	cast on
k	knit
k2tog	knit two together
kfb	knit into front and back of stitch
p	purl
pm	place marker
ssk	slip, slip, knit slipped stitches together
st[s]	stitch[es]

Body

Using teal yarn, CO 6, pm join to knit in the round. Split stitches evenly between 3 needles.

Round 1: Kfb 6 times. 12 sts

Round 2 and all even numbered rounds: Knit.

Round 3: (Kfb, k1) 6 times. 18 sts

Round 5: (Kfb, k2) 6 times. 24 sts

Round 7: (Kfb, k3) 6 times. 30 sts

Round 9: (Kfb, k4) 6 times. 36 sts

Round 11: (Kfb, k5) 6 times. 42 sts

Rounds 12–14: Knit.

Round 15: (K2tog, k5) 6 times. 36 sts

Rounds 16–18: Knit.

Round 19: (K2tog, k4) 6 times. 30 sts

Round 20: Knit.

Switch to light blue yarn.

Rounds 21–26: Knit.

Round 27: (K2tog, k3) 6 times. 24 sts

Round 28–29: Knit.

Round 30: (K2tog, k2) 6 times. 18 sts

Bind off.

Head

Using light blue yarn, CO 6, pm join to knit in the round. Split stitches evenly between 3 needles.

Round 1: Kfb 6 times. 12 sts

Round 2 and all even numbered rounds: Knit.

Round 3: (Kfb, k1) 6 times. 18 sts

Round 5: (Kfb, k2) 6 times. 24 sts

Round 7: (Kfb, k3) 6 times. 30 sts

Round 9: (Kfb, k4) 6 times. 36 sts

Round 11: (Kfb, k5) 6 times. 42 sts

Rounds 12–20: Knit.

Round 21: (K2tog, k5) 6 times. 36 sts

Round 22 and all even numbered rounds: Knit.

Round 23: (K2tog, k4) 6 times. 30 sts

Round 25: (K2tog, k3) 6 times. 24 sts

Round 27: (K2tog, k2) 6 times. 18 sts

Bind off.

Legs (knit 2)

Using teal yarn, CO 5, pm join to knit in the round.

Round 1: Kfb 5 times. 10 sts

Round 2: (Kfb, k1) 5 times. 15 sts

Round 3: (Kfb, k2) 5 times. 20 sts

Rounds 4–7: Knit.

Round 8: (K2tog, k2) 5 times. 15 sts

Knit 18 rounds. Bind off.

Arms (knit 2)

Using light blue yarn, CO 5, pm join to knit in the round.

Round 1: Kfb 5 times. 10 sts

Round 2: (Kfb, k1) 5 times. 15 sts

Rounds 3–4: Knit.

Round 5: (K2tog, k1) 5 times. 10 sts

Knit 15 rounds. Bind off.

Ears (knit 2)

Using two US 7 (4.5mm) needles and light blue yarn, CO 4.

Row 1: Purl.

Row 2: K1, kfb twice, k1. 6 sts

Rows 3–7: Complete in stockinette st.

Row 8: K1, Kfb, k2, kfb, k1. 8 sts

Row 9: Purl.

Row 10: K1, Kfb, k4, kfb, k1. 10 sts

Row 11: Purl.

Row 12: K1, k2tog, k4, ssk, k1. 8 sts

Row 13: Purl.

Row 14: K1, k2tog, k2, ssk, k1. 6 sts

Row 15–17: Complete in stockinette st.

Row 18: K1, k2tog, ssk, k1. 4 sts
Row 19: Purl.
Row 20: K2tog, ssk. 2 sts
Break yarn, pull tail through remaining sts
and weave end into purl side of ear.

Assembly

Stuff head and body firmly. Center head
on body. Seam together using ladder
stitch.

Stuff legs and arms lightly. Center legs
on bottom front of body and seam using
ladder stitch.

Flatten top of arms slightly and seam to
side of body using ladder stitch.

Press ears lightly. Trace onto white felt,
and cut out, leaving a ¼ in. margin.
Attach felt lining to purl side of ears
using contrasting thread and a blanket
stitch. Sew ears to top of head using
mattress stitch.

Cut felt pieces for face using template.
Center eyes on head. Sew on using
contrasting thread and blanket stitch,
beginning with black, followed by white,
blue, then pupil, and white flecks. Center
mouth between eyes on face. Sew on
using contrasting thread.

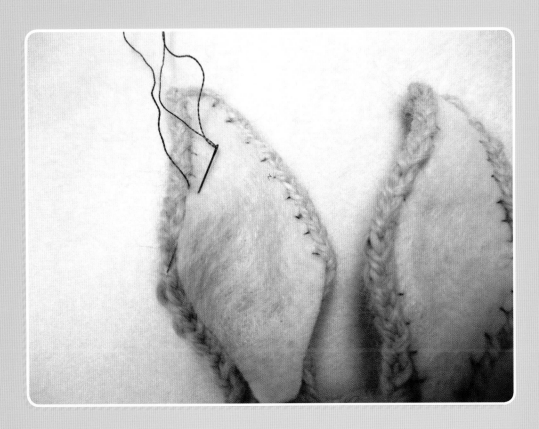

 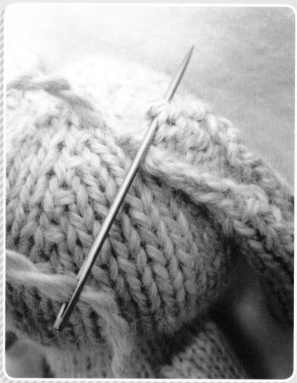

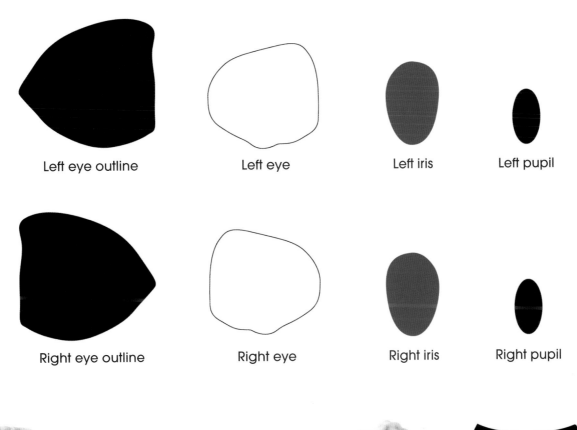

Left eye outline

Left eye

Left iris

Left pupil

Right eye outline

Right eye

Right iris

Right pupil

Mouth

CUTE COULD BE MY MIDDLE NAME. BUT IT'S WARREN.

Rosie

Rosie was inspired by the phrase "the elephant in the room". I always thought that was such an odd expression. If there were an elephant in my room, particularly a purple one wearing a fabulous crown, I'd talk of nothing else. I'd tell everyone. Some secrets are just too good to keep to yourself.

Materials

- 1 skein Cascade 220 in 9453
- 1 set US 7 (4.5) double pointed needles
- Scraps of wool felt in white, black and light pink, and purple
- Toy stuffing
- Yarn needle
- Embroidery needle
- Thread

Glossary of abbreviations

CO	cast on
k	knit
k2tog	knit two together
kfb	knit into front and back of stitch
pm	place marker
ssk	slip, slip, knit slipped stitches together
st[s]	stitch[es]

Body

CO 6, pm join to knit in the round. Split stitches evenly between 3 needles.
Round 1: Kfb 6 times. 12 sts
Round 2 and all even numbered rounds: Knit.
Round 3: (Kfb, k1) 6 times. 18 sts
Round 5: (Kfb, k2) 6 times. 24 sts
Round 7: (Kfb, k3) 6 times. 30 sts
Round 9: (Kfb, k4) 6 times. 36 sts
Round 11: (Kfb, k5) 6 times. 42 sts
Rounds 12–23: Knit.
Round 24: (K2tog, k5) 6 times. 36 sts
Rounds 25–27: Knit.
Round 28: (K2tog, k4) 6 times. 30 sts
Round 29: Knit.
Round 30: (K2tog, k3) 6 times. 24 sts
Round 31: Knit.
Round 32: (K2tog, k2) 6 times. 18 sts
Bind off.

Head

CO 10, pm, join to knit in the round.
Rounds 1–10: Knit.
Round 11: K2, kfb, k4, kfb, k2. 12 sts
Round 12: K1, kfb, k1, kfb, k4, kfb, k1, kfb, k1. 16 sts
Round 13: K5, kfb, k4, kfb, k5. 18 sts
Round 14: K1, kfb, k4, kfb, k4, kfb, k4, kfb, k1. 22 sts
Round 15: K8, kfb, k4, kfb, k8. 24 sts
Round 16: K1, kfb, k7, kfb, k4, kfb, k7, kfb, k1. 28 sts
Round 17: K11, kfb, k4, kfb, k11. 30 sts
Round 18: K1, kfb, k10, kfb, k4, kfb, k10, kfb, k1. 34 sts
Round 19: K14, kfb, k4, kfb, k14. 36 sts
Rounds 20–28: Knit.
Round 29: (K2tog, k4) 6 times. 30 sts
Round 30 and all even numbered rounds: Knit.
Round 31: (K2tog, k3) 6 times. 24 sts
Pause and stuff head nearly full.
Round 33: (K2tog, k2) 6 times. 18 sts
Round 35: (K2tog, k1) 6 times. 12 sts
Round 37: K2tog 6 times. 6 sts
Break yarn. Pull tail through remaining stitches. Pull tight, knot and pull tail to inside of toy.

Legs (knit 2)

CO 5, pm join to knit in the round.
Round 1: Kfb 5 times. 10 sts
Round 2: (Kfb, k1) 5 times. 15 sts
Round 3: (Kfb, k2) 5 times. 20 sts
Round 4: (Kfb, k3) 5 times. 25 sts
Round 5: Knit.
Round 6: K2tog, k21, ssk. 23 sts

Round 7 and all odd numbered rounds: Knit.
Round 8: K2tog, k19, ssk. 21 sts
Round 10: K2tog, k17, ssk. 19 sts
Round 12: K2tog, k15, ssk. 17 sts
Bind off.

Arms (knit 2)

CO 5, pm join to knit in the round.
Round 1: Kfb 5 times. 10 sts
Round 2: (Kfb, k1) 5 times. 15 sts
Rounds 3–4: Knit.
Round 5: (K2tog, k1) 5 times. 10 sts
Knit 6 rounds. Bind off.

Assembly

Stuff body and head firmly. Center head on top of body with trunk pointing down. Seam using ladder stitch.

Stuff legs firmly. Center on front of body. Seam using ladder stitch.

Flatten tops of arms slightly. Center on sides of body and seam into place using ladder stitch.

Cut felt pieces from template. Center small purple circle over snout. Use thread from cast on edge to sew opening shut.

Curl the crown to form a circle. Stitch side into place with thread, then use thread to secure to top of head.

Center eyes to side of body, and attach one piece at a time using thread and blanket stitch.

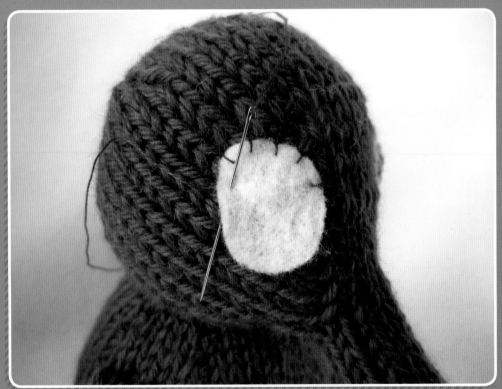

Crown

 Eye (2)

 Iris (2)

 Pupil (2)

 Snout

ELEPHANT IN THE HOUSE, YO!

Cyclops

It would be so lonely to be a monster. Imagine trying to make new friends when you only have one eye. Everywhere you go, you're greeted by stares of awkward curiosity, or worse, fear. This cyclops took a proactive approach to his isolated existence. Everyone loves bunnies, so why not wear a bunny suit? Even with one eye, he's infinitely more huggable.

Materials

- 1 skein Cascade 220 in 0980 (green)
- 1 skein Cascade 220 in 7815 (light blue)
- 1 set US 6 (4mm) double pointed needles
- 1 pair US 6 (4mm) straight needles
- Small amount of contrasting yarn for stitching (I used orange)
- Small scraps of felt in white, blue, light blue, and black
- Yarn needle
- Embroidery needle
- Toy stuffing

Glossary of abbreviations

BO	bind off
CO	cast on
k	knit
k2tog	knit two together
kfb	knit into front and back of stitch
p	purl
pfb	purl into front and back of stitch
pm	place marker
ssk	slip, slip, knit slipped stitches together
st[s]	stitch[es]

Body (knit from the bottom up)
Using US 6 (4mm) double pointed needles and green yarn, CO 6, pm, join to knit in the round.
Round 1: Kfb 6 times. 12 sts
Round 2 and all even numbered rounds through 14: Knit.
Round 3: (Kfb, k1) 6 times. 18 sts
Round 5: (Kfb, k2) 6 times. 24 sts
Round 7: (Kfb, k3) 6 times. 30 sts
Round 9: (Kfb, k4) 6 times. 36 sts
Round 11: (Kfb, k5) 6 times. 42 sts
Round 13: (Kfb, k6) 6 times. 48 sts
Round 15: (Kfb, k7) 6 times. 54 sts
Rounds 16–27: Knit.
Round 28: K8, k2tog, k7, ssk, k16, k2tog, k7, ssk, k8. 50 sts
Round 29: K7, k2tog, k7, ssk, k14, k2tog, k7, ssk, k7. 46 sts
Round 30: K6, k2tog, k7, ssk, k12, k2tog, k7, ssk, k6. 42 sts
Round 31: K5, k2tog, k7, ssk, k10, k2tog, k7, ssk, k5. 38 sts
Round 32: K4, k2tog, k7, ssk, k8, k2tog, k7, ssk, k4. 34 sts
Rounds 33–38: Knit.

Begin division for face opening:
Round 39: K14, BO 6, k14. 28 sts
Round 40: K12, k2tog, turn, p13, move marker, p12, p2tog. 26 sts
Row 41: K2tog, k11, move marker, k11, k2tog. 24 sts
Rows 42–43: Complete in stockinette, moving marker to keep center marked.
Row 44: Pfb, p11, move marker, p11, pfb. 26 sts
Row 45: Kfb, k12, move marker, k12, kfb. 28 sts
Row 46: P14, move marker, p14, CO 6. 34 sts
Rejoin to knit in the round. Purl remaining 14 sts to marker.
Rounds 47–50: Knit.
Round 51: K3, k2tog, ssk, k3, k2tog, ssk, k6, k2tog, ssk, k3, k2tog, ssk, k3. 26 sts
Round 52: Knit.
Round 53: K2, k2tog, ssk, k1, k2tog, ssk, k4, k2tog, ssk, k1, k2tog, ssk, k2. 18 sts
Round 54: Knit.
Round 55: K1, k2tog, k3, ssk, k2, k2tog, k3, ssk, k1. 14 sts
Round 56: K2tog 7 times. 7 sts

Break yarn, pull tail through remaining stitches, knot, pull to inside of toy. Stuff body mostly full through face opening.

Face
Using US 6 (4mm) straight needles and blue yarn, CO 8.
Row 1: Kfb, k7. 9 sts
Row 2: Pfb, p8. 10 sts
Row 3: Kfb, k9. 11 sts
Row 4: Pfb, p10. 12 sts
Rows 5–8: Complete in stockinette st.
Row 9: K2tog, k10. 11 sts
Row 10: P2tog, p9. 10 sts
Row 11: K2tog, k8. 9 sts
Row 12: P2tog, p7. 8 sts
Bind off.

Legs (make 2)

Using US 6 (4mm) double pointed needles and blue yarn, CO 5, pm, join to knit in the round.

Round 1: Kfb 5 times. 10 sts
Round 2: (Kfb, k1) 5 times. 15 sts
Round 3: (Kfb, k2) 5 times. 20 sts
Round 4: (Kfb, k3) 5 times. 25 sts
Round 5: Knit.
Switch to green yarn.
Knit 9 rounds.
Round 15: K2tog, k11, k2tog, k10. 23 sts
Knit 8 rounds.
Bind off, leaving a 9 in. tail.

Arms (make 2)

Using US 6 (4mm) double pointed needles and blue yarn, CO 5, pm, join to knit in the round.

Round 1: Kfb 5 times. 10 sts
Round 2: (Kfb, k1) 5 times. 15 sts
Knit 2 rounds. Switch to green yarn.
Knit 8 rounds.
Round 13: K2tog, k13. 14 sts
Knit 7 rounds.
Bind off, leaving a 9 in. tail.

Ears (make 2)

Using US 6 (4mm) straight needles and green yarn, CO 4.

Rows 1–5: Complete in stockinette st.
Row 6: K1, kfb twice, k1. 6 sts
Rows 7–9: Knit.
Row 10: K1, kfb, k2, kfb, k1. 8 sts
Row 11: K, k2tog, k2, ssk, k1. 6 sts
Rows 12–14: Knit.
Row 15: K1, k2tog, ssk, k1. 4 sts
Rows 16–18: Knit.
Row 19: K2tog twice. 2 sts
Break yarn, pull tail through sts. Weave end into purl side of ear.

Assembly

Face

Center face in opening on body. Using scrap of green yarn, sew through opening into face behind with a running stitch. Stretch face firmly as you go, pausing to stuff full before finishing seam. Using contrasting orange yarn and running stitch, trace the opening around the face. Continue the line down the front of the body as shown to create a faux zipper. Cut eye pieces from felt using template. Use orange thread and blanket stitch to sew eye to face starting with the white, followed by the iris in dark blue, and then the pupil.

Arms and legs

Stuff legs firmly. Use scrap of orange yarn and a running stitch to sew around the division between green and blue. Attach to bottom of body using ladder stitch. Repeat for arms, stuffing less firmly, and sewing to sides of body.

Ears

Press ears lightly. Lay flat of a piece of light blue felt and trace. Cut, subtracting an 1/8 in. border around perimeter. Use orange thread and blanket stitch to sew felt to the purl side of the ears. Sew ears to top of head using green yarn and ladder stitch.

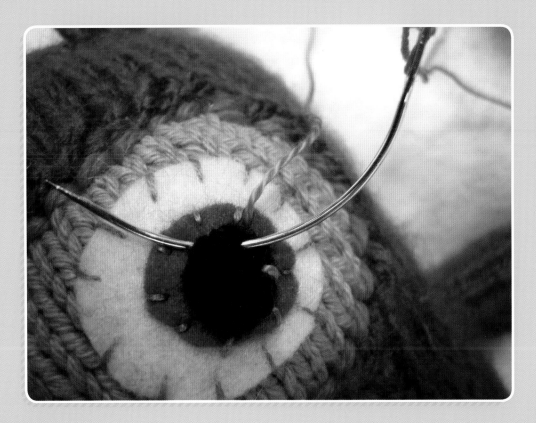

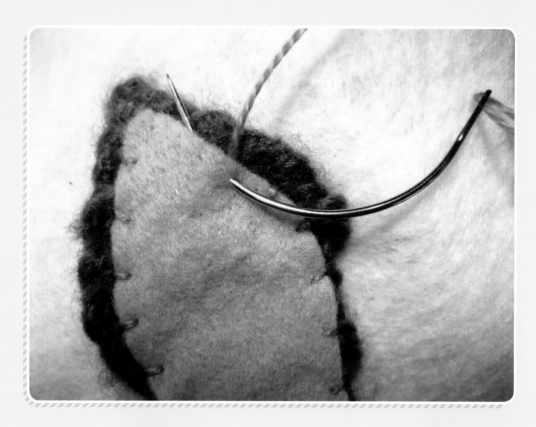

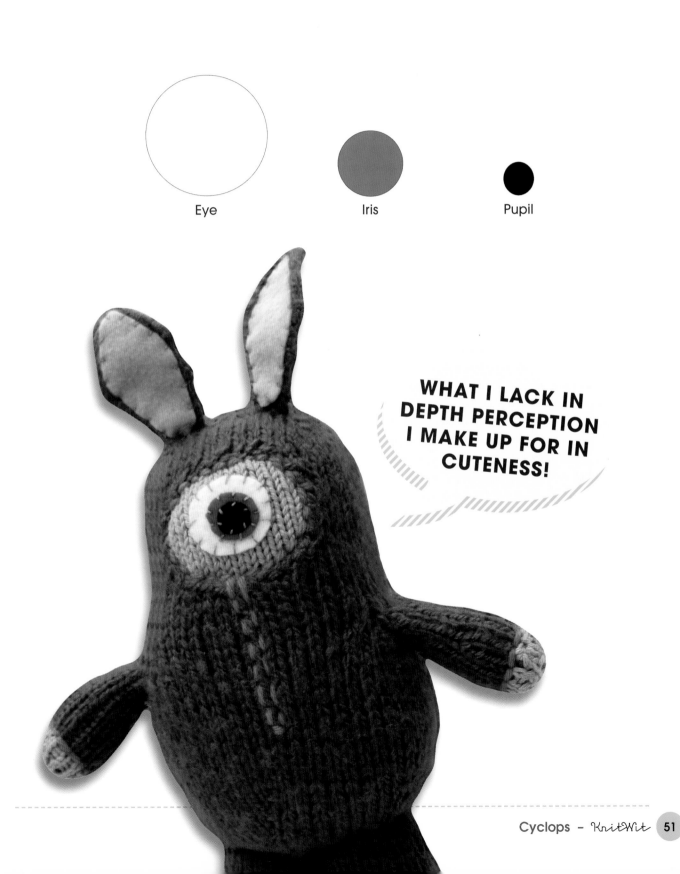

Eye

Iris

Pupil

WHAT I LACK IN DEPTH PERCEPTION I MAKE UP FOR IN CUTENESS!

Jacques Crusteau

Jacques was inspired by a trip to the grocery store, where I watched my daughter have an imaginary conversation with the lobsters in the tank by the seafood counter. For her, even something as odd and spiny as a lobster is cute and friendworthy. When I finished the toy, Sophia was elated. In our house, Jacques lives the good life. He joins us for dinner, sleeps in a big comfy bed, and even goes on vacation.

Materials

- 1 skein Cascade 220 Quatro in Madagascar [MC]
- 1 skein Cascade 220 in White [CC]
- 1 set US 6 (4mm) double pointed needles
- Toy stuffing
- Yarn needle
- Embroidery needle
- 2 pieces of black felt cut in ½ in. circles

Glossary of abbreviations

CO	cast on
k	knit
k2tog	knit two together
kfb	knit into front and back of stitch
pm	place marker
ssk	slip, slip, knit slipped stitches together
st[s]	stitch[es]
yo	yarn over

Head
Using MC, CO 5, pm, join to knit in the round.
Round 1: Kfb 5 times. 10 sts
Round 2: (Kfb, k1) 5 times. 15 sts
Round 3: (Kfb, k2) 5 times. 20 sts
Round 4: Knit.
Round 5: Kfb, k3, (kfb twice, k3) 3 times, kfb. 28 sts
Rounds 6–7: Knit.
Round 8: Kfb, k5, (kfb twice, k5) 3 times, kfb. 36 sts
Rounds 9–10: Knit.
Round 11: Kfb, k7, (kfb twice, k7) 3 times, kfb. 44 sts
Rounds 12–13: Knit.
Round 14: Kfb, k9, (kfb twice, k9) 3 times, kfb. 52 sts
Rounds 15–16: Knit.
Round 17: Kfb, k11, (kfb twice, k11) 3 times, kfb. 60 sts
Rounds 18–19: Knit.
Round 20: Kfb, k13, (kfb twice, k13) 3 times, kfb. 68 sts
Rounds 21–25: Knit.
Round 26: (K2tog, k13, ssk) 4 times. 60 sts

Round 27: Knit.
Round 28: (K2tog, k11, ssk) 4 times. 52 sts
Round 29: Knit.
Round 30: (K2tog, k9, ssk) 4 times. 44 sts
Continue decreasing in this manner every row until 20 sts remain. Break yarn, pull tail through remaining stitches. Stuff head firmly.

Body
Using MC, CO 16, pm, join to knit in the round.
Round 1: K4, kfb, k2, kfb, k4, kfb, k2, kfb. 20 sts
Round 2: Kfb, k2, kfb twice, k4, kfb twice, k2, kfb twice, k4, kfb. 28 sts
Round 3: K6, (kfb, k6) 3 times, kfb. 32 sts
Round 4: Kfb, k4, kfb twice, k8, kfb twice, k4, kfb twice, k8, kfb. 40 sts
Round 5: K8, kfb, k10, kfb, k8, kfb, k10, kfb. 44 sts
Rounds 6–12: Knit.
Round 13: K8, k2tog, k10, ssk, k8, k2tog, k10, ssk. 40 sts

Rounds 14–17: Knit.
Round 18: K2tog, k4, ssk, k2tog, k8, ssk, k2tog, k4, ssk, k2tog, k8, ssk. 32 sts
Round 19: Knit.
Round 20: K6, k2tog, k6, ssk, k6, k2tog, k6, ssk. 28 sts
Round 21: Knit.
Round 22: K2tog, k2, ssk, k2tog, k4, ssk, k2tog, k2, ssk, k2tog, k4, ssk. 20 sts
Bind off. Stuff firmly.

Tail
Using MC, CO 16, pm, join to knit in the round.
Round 1: (K4, kfb, k2, kfb) twice. 20 sts
Round 2: (K4, kfb, k4, kfb) twice. 24 sts
Round 3: (K4, kfb, k6, kfb) twice. 28 sts
Round 4: (K4, kfb, k8, kfb) twice. 32 sts
Round 5: (K4, kfb, k10, kfb) twice. 36 sts
Rounds 6–10: Knit.
Round 11: (K4, k2tog, k10, ssk) twice. 32 sts
Round 12: (K4, k2tog, k8, ssk) twice. 28 sts

Round 13: (K4, k2tog, k6, ssk) twice. 24 sts

Round 14: (K4, k2tog, k4, ssk) twice. 20 sts

Round 15: (K4, kfb, k4, kfb) twice. 24 sts

Round 16: (K4, kfb, k6, kfb) twice. 28 sts

Round 17: (K4, kfb, k8, kfb) twice. 32 sts

Rounds 18–21: Knit.

Round 22: (K4, k2tog, k8, ssk) twice. 28 sts

Round 23: (K4, k2tog, k6, ssk) twice. 24 sts

Round 24: (K4, k2tog, k4, ssk) twice. 20 sts

Round 25: (K4, kfb, k4, kfb) twice. 24 sts

Round 26: (K4, kfb, k6, kfb) twice. 28 sts

Rounds 27–29: Knit.

Round 30: (K4, k2tog, k6, ssk) twice. 24 sts

Round 31: (K4, k2tog, k4, ssk) twice. 20 sts

Round 32: (K4, k2tog, k2, ssk) twice. 16 sts

Round 33: (K4, kfb, k2, kfb) twice. 20 sts

Round 34: (K4, kfb, k4, kfb) twice. 24 sts

Rounds 35–36: Knit.

Round 37: (K4, k2tog, k4, ssk) twice. 20 sts

Round 38: (K2tog, ssk, k2tog, k2, ssk) twice. 12 sts

Round 39: Knit.

Round 40: K2, kfb, k2, kfb, k2, kfb, k2, kfb. 16 sts

Round 41 and all remaining odd numbered rounds: Knit.

Round 42: (K2, kfb, k4, kfb) twice. 20 sts

Round 43: (K2, kfb, k6, kfb) twice. 24 sts

Continue increasing in this manner until there are 40 sts.

Next round: K1, yo, (k2tog, k2, yo) 9 times, k2tog, k1.

Knit 2 rounds even. Bind off leaving a 12 in. tail. Using a yarn needle, and the tail, fold over the open end to reveal scalloped edge. Stitch in place around the inside of the toy. Stuff tail firmly, but not so firmly that the indentations in the tail disappear.

Fold bottom of tail in half. Stitch along the bottom using a mattress stitch, pulling tight inside the scallops to accentuate.

Claw (make 2)

Large half

Using MC, CO 4, divide between two needles, pm, join to knit in the round.

Round 1: K1, kfb twice, k1. 6 sts

Round 2: K2, kfb twice, k2. 8 sts

Round 3: K3, kfb twice, k3. 10 sts

Round 4: K4, kfb twice, k4. 12 sts

Round 5: K5, kfb twice, k5. 14 sts

Round 6: Knit.

Round 7: K2tog, k4, kfb twice, k4, ssk.

Round 8: Knit.

Round 9: K6, kfb twice, k6. 16 sts

Round 10: Knit.

Round 11: K7, kfb twice, k7. 18 sts

Round 12: Knit.

Round 13: K8, kfb twice, k8. 20 sts

Round 14: Knit.

Round 15: K9, kfb twice, k9. 22 sts

Round 16–19: Knit.

Round 20: K9, ssk, k2tog, k9. 20 sts

Round 21: Knit.

Round 22: K8, ssk, k2tog, k8. 18 sts

Round 23: Knit.

Round 24: Kfb, k6, ssk, k2tog, k6, kfb. Place stitches on a piece of scrap yarn.

Small half

Round 1: K1, kfb twice, k1. 6 sts

Round 2: K2, kfb twice, k2. 8 sts

Round 3: K3, kfb twice, k3. 10 sts

Round 4: Knit.

Round 5: K4, kfb twice, k4. 12 sts

Round 6: Knit.

Round 7: K5, kfb twice, k5. 14 sts

Rounds 8–13: Knit.

Round 14: K5, ssk, k2tog, k5. 12 sts

Rounds 15–19: Knit.

Round 20: K4, ssk, k2tog, k4. 10 sts

Rounds 21–23: Knit.

Round 24: Kfb, k2, ssk, k2tog, k2, kfb.

Break yarn. Weave ends on both sides of claw to inside. Stuff each side of claw mostly full. Carefully remove scrap yarn and place slide stitches onto the needles alongside the small half of the claw as shown.

Reconnect yarn on edge of small half. 28 sts

Stuff the claw as you go.

Round 25–26: Knit.

Round 27: (K2tog, k10, ssk) twice. 24 sts

Rounds 28: Knit.

Round 29: (K2tog, k8, ssk) twice. 20 sts

Rounds 30–33: Knit.

Round 34: (K2tog, k6, ssk) twice. 16 sts

Rounds 35–38: Knit.

Round 39: (K2tog, k4, ssk) twice. 12 sts

Rounds 40–56: Knit.

Round 57: (K2tog, k2, ssk) twice. 8 sts

Bind off.

Stuff claw completely full.

Eyes (make 2)

Using CC, CO 5, pm, join to knit in the round.

Round 1: Kfb 5 times. 10 sts

Round 2: (Kfb, k1) 5 times. 15 sts

Round 3: (Kfb, k2) 5 times. 20 sts

Round 4: (Kfb, k3) 5 times. 25 sts

Round 5: Knit.

Round 6: (Kfb, k4) 5 times. 30 sts

Knit 6 rounds. Bind off.

Assembly

Using a piece of MC and a ladder stitch, center head on top of body and attach. Use the same method to attach the tail. For the arms, cut a scrap of MC 10 in. long, and knot the end. Insert at the top of the arm on the small claw side, and weave yarn in and out of side, pulling as you go to curve the arm. Knot to secure, and pull to inside of toy. Use ladder stitch to attach arms to side of body.

For the eyes, use a scrap of CC, center eyes near the front of the head, spacing them a ¼ in. apart. Use a ladder stitch to secure, stuffing the eyes when the stitching is ¾ complete.

Attach pupils using a piece of black thread and mattress stitch.

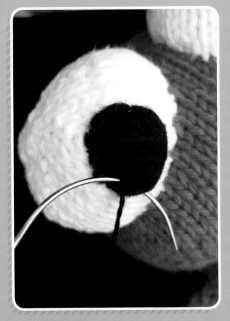

Mr. Abominable

Mr Abominable was the most obvious choice of monster to knit this winter. While suffering through the worst winter in recorded history, I sat huddled under a quilt on the couch with my needles, occasionally catching a glimpse out the window of Mr. Abominable himself, shoveling my driveway for me. Of course, that could have been my kind and helpful landlord. With that kind of wind and snow, everyone winds up looking like a yeti.

Materials

- 1 set US 7 (4.5mm) double pointed needles
- 1 skein Cascade 220 wool in 8010 (white)
- 1 skein Cascade 220 wool in 9476 (beige)
- Small pieces of felt in peach, white, blue, and black
- Toy stuffing
- Yarn needle
- Embroidery needle
- Black embroidery floss

Glossary of abbreviations

CO	cast on
k	knit
k2tog	knit two together
kfb	knit into front and back of stitch
p	purl
p2tog	purl two together
pm	place marker
ssk	slip, slip, knit slipped stitches together
st[s]	stitch[es]

Legs (make 2)

Using white yarn, CO 20, pm, join to knit in the round.

Rounds 1–2: Knit.

Round 3: Kfb, k19. 21 sts

Continue increasing 1 stitch at the beginning of the round, every third round, until you have 24 sts.

Begin shaping for crotch.

Row 13: K2tog, k20, ssk. 22 sts

Row 14: Turn, p2tog, p18, p2tog. 20 sts

Row 15: Knit.

Continue in stockinette st for 4 more rows. Place stitches on a piece of contrasting yarn. Cut working yarn, weave end into fabric. Repeat for second leg. (When making the second leg, leave the working yarn attached to begin body.)

Seam the legs together at crotch, beginning and ending just below stitch on scrap yarn.

Move stitches from scrap yarn back to the needles. Beginning next to seam with working yarn, divide evenly among needles.

Body

Pm, knit in the round.

Round 1: Knit. 40 sts

Round 2: K6, kfb, k6, kfb twice, k10, kfb twice, k6, kfb, k6. 46 sts

Round 3: Knit.

Round 4: K6, kfb, k8, kfb twice, k12, kfb twice, k8, kfb, k6. 52 sts

Round 5: Knit.

Round 6: K17, kfb twice, k14, kfb twice, k17. 56 sts

Rounds 7–12: Knit.

Round 13: K17, ssk, k2tog, k14, ssk, k2tog, k17. 52 sts

Rounds 14–20: Knit.

Round 21: K18, k2tog, k12, ssk, k18. 50 sts

Rounds 22–24: Knit.

Round 25: K16, ssk, k14, k2tog, k16. 48 sts

Rounds 26–43: Knit.

Round 44: K15, ssk, k2tog, k10, ssk, k2tog, k15. 44 sts

Round 45 and all odd numbered rounds: Knit.

Round 46: K4, ssk, k10, k2tog, k8, ssk, k10, k2tog, k4. 40 sts

Round 48: K3, ssk, (k2tog, k6, ssk) 3 times, k2tog, k3. 32 sts

Round 50: K2, ssk, (k2tog, k4, ssk) 3 times, k2tog, k2. 24 sts

Pause and stuff toy mostly full.

Round 52: K1, ssk, (k2tog, k2, ssk) 3 times, k2tog, k1. 16 sts

Round 54: Ssk, (k2tog, ssk) 3 times, k2tog. 8 sts

Cut yarn, pull tail through remaining stitches, knot, and pull knot to inside of toy. Finish stuffing toy through leg holes.

Arms (make 2)

Using white yarn, CO 15, pm, join to knit in the round.

Rounds 1–3: Knit.

Round 4: Kfb, k14. 16 sts

Continue to increase 1 stitch at the beginning on every fourth round until there are 20 sts. Bind off.

Hands (make 2)

Using beige yarn, single-stranded, CO 18, pm, join to knit in the round.

Rounds 1–3: Knit.

Round 4: K2tog, k5, ssk, k2tog, k5, ssk. 14 sts

Round 5: Knit.

Round 6: K2tog, k3, ssk, k2tog, k3, ssk. 10 sts

Round 7: K2tog, k1, ssk, k2tog, k1, ssk. 6 sts

Break yarn, pull tail through remaining stitches, knot, and pull to inside of toy.

Feet (make 2)

Begin toes

Using beige yarn, CO 4, place 2 stitches on each needle, pm, join to knit in the round. Knit one round. Leave stitches on 2 needles. Break yarn, leaving 4 inch tail.

Repeat between *s 3 more times. Slide each toe onto the original 2 needles with the first toe as shown. Knot together the tails from the needle end of each toe to the tail next to it. Cut tails short. You will knit the feet around the loose strands.

Reattach yarn to edge of foot. Pm, begin working in the round. Knit 8 rounds. Bind off. Using a yarn needle, pull tails from cast on edge of toe to the inside of the foot. Stuff the foot lightly. Sew open edge shut using mattress seam.

Assembly

Legs

Stuff ends of legs firmly. Center each foot under leg, inserting slightly into back of leg. Use white yarn and running stitch to sew foot into leg hole.

Arms

Insert hand into large end of arm. Use white yarn and sew through the arm into hand to attach.

Stuff arm and hand, firmly at bottom, and loosely at top. Flatten top of arm, and use ladder stitch to attach to side of body.

Face

Cut out felt pieces using templates. Attach face first, using black embroidery floss and blanket stitch. Then attach irises, pupils, and eyebrows.

Finally, embroider frown (or smile!) using a running stitch.

 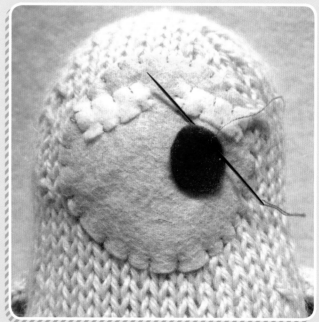

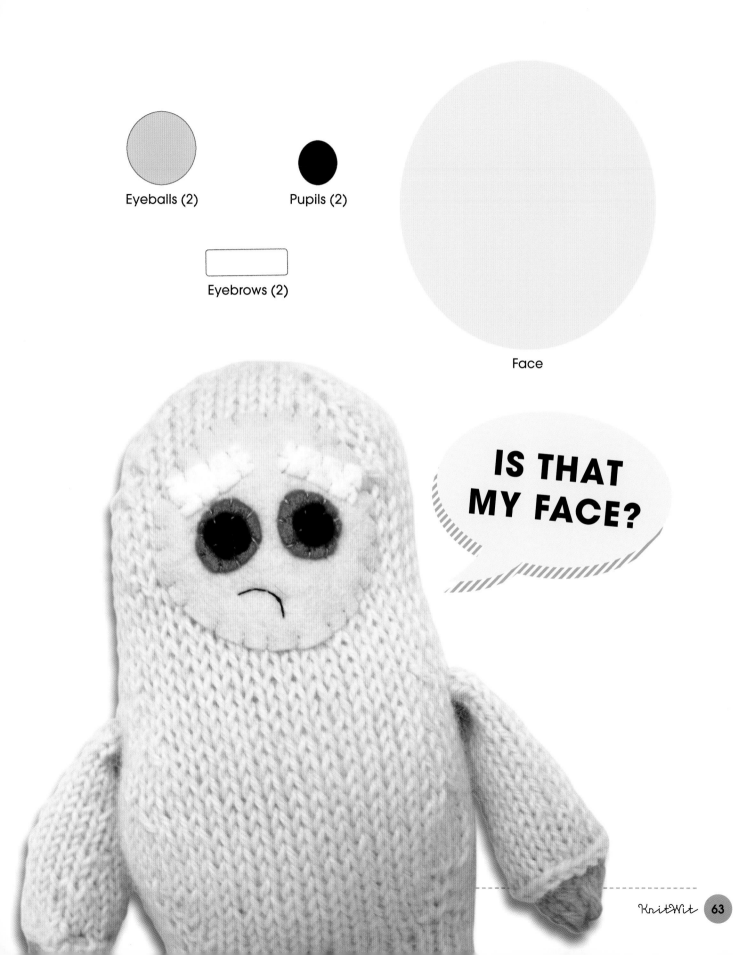

Eyeballs (2)

Pupils (2)

Eyebrows (2)

Face

IS THAT
MY FACE?

Peg

Peg was knitted as a trade for some photography work. My friend Jamie generously photographed some of my art, and I wanted to create something that would make her laugh. I'm not sure if it was my own childhood fascination with pirates, or the hours of watching Spongebob Squarepants with my children that led me to create him, but who doesn't love a three-eyed pink swashbuckler? I can assure you he is as ferocious as he looks.

Materials

- For upper body and eyes, 1 skein Cascade 220 wool in 9493 (salmon)
- For pants, 1 skein Cascade 220 wool in 8400 (gray)
- For belt, 1 skein Cascade 220 wool in 8555 (black)
- For peg leg, 1 skein Cascade 220 wool in 9476 (beige)
- 1 set US 6 (4 mm) double pointed needles
- Toy stuffing
- Yarn needle
- Scraps of felt in black (eye patch), white (teeth), gray (sword blade), maize (gold tooth), medium green (eyes), and tan (sword handle and belt buckle)
- Thread in white, maize, brown, and black

Glossary of abbreviations

CO	cast on
k	knit
k2tog	knit two together
kfb	knit into front and back of stitch
pm	place marker
ssk	slip, slip, knit, slipped stitches together
st[s]	stitch[es]

Body

Start at the hips (the right leg and peg leg are made and attached later).
Using the pants color (gray) yarn, CO 5 stitches, pm, and join to knit in the round.
Round 1: Kfb 5 times. 10 sts
Round 2: (kfb, k1) 5 times. 15 sts
Round 3: (kfb, k2) 5 times. 20 sts
Round 4: (kfb, k3) 5 times. 25 sts
Round 5: (kfb, k4) 5 times. 30 sts
Round 6: (kfb, k5) 5 times. 35 sts
Round 7: (kfb, k6) 5 times. 40 sts
Round 8: (kfb, k7) 5 times. 45 sts
Round 9: (kfb, k8) 5 times. 50 sts
Round 10: (kfb, k9) 5 times. 55 sts
Round 11: (kfb, k10) 5 times. 60 sts
Rounds 12–14: Knit.
Change to the belt color (black) yarn.
Rounds 15–20 Knit.
Change to the body color (salmon) yarn.
Round 21: K8, k2tog, k7, ssk, k5, k2tog, k8, ssk, k5, k2tog, k7, ssk, k8. 54 sts
Round 22 and every even-numbered round through round 28: Knit.
Round 23: K21, k2tog, k8, ssk, k21. 52 sts
Round 25: K7, k2tog, k7, ssk, k3, k2tog, k6, ssk, k3, k2tog, k7, ssk, k7. 46 sts
Round 27: K17, k2tog, k8, ssk, k17. 44 sts
Round 29: K6, k2tog, k6, ssk, k12, k2tog, k6, ssk, k6. 40 sts
Rounds 30–31: Knit
Round 32: K5, k2tog, k6, ssk, k10, k2tog, k6, ssk, k5. 36 sts
Rounds 33–34: Knit.
Round 35: K4, k2tog, k6, ssk, k8, k2tog, k6, ssk, k4. 32 sts
Rounds 36–37: Knit.
Round 38: K3, k2tog, k6, ssk, k6, k2tog, k6, ssk, k3. 28 sts
Rounds 39–40: Knit.
Pause at this point to stuff the body almost to the top.
Round 42: K2, k2tog, k6, ssk, k4, k2tog, k6, ssk, k2. 24 sts
Round 43: K1, k2tog, k6, ssk, k2, k2tog, k6, ssk, k1. 20 sts
Round 44: K2tog, k6, ssk, k2tog, k6, ssk. 16 sts
Round 45: k2tog 8 times. 8 sts
Stuff the body to the top. Cut the yarn leaving a tail of 7 inches. Pull the tail through the remaining 8 stitches, knot, and pull the knot into the body.

Eyes (make 3)

Using the body color (salmon) yarn, CO 12 stitches, pm, join to knit in the round.
Round 1: Knit
Round 2: kfb, k2, kfb, k2, kfb, k2, kfb, k2. 16 sts
Round 3: kfb, k4, kfb, k2, kfb, k4, kfb, k2. 20 sts
Rounds 4–10: Knit.
Round 11: ssk, k4, k2tog, k2, ssk, k4, k2tog, k2. 16 sts
Round 12: ssk, k2, k2tog, k2, ssk, k2, k2tog, k2. 12 sts
Round 13: ssk, k2tog twice, ssk, k2tog twice. 6 sts

Cut the yarn leaving a tail of 7 inches. Pull the tail through the remaining 6 stitches, knot, and pull the knot inside of the eye. Stuff the eye.

Arm (make 2)

Start at the top of the arm.
Using the body color (salmon) yarn, CO 5 stitches, pm, join to knit in the round.
Round 1: kfb 5 times. 10 sts
Round 2: (kfb, k1) 5 times. 15 sts
Round 3: (kfb, k2) 5 times. 20 sts
Rounds 4–5: Knit.
Round 6: (k2tog, k2) 5 times. 15 sts
Round 7: K2tog, k11, k2tog. 13 sts
Round 8: K2tog, k9, k2tog. 11 sts
Knit 14 rows. Bind off.
Stuff the arms, filling them more firmly in the hands (if you can call them hands).

Right Leg

Start at the top of the leg.
Using the pants color (gray) yarn, CO 5 stitches, pm, join to knit in the round.
Round 1: kfb 5 times. 10 sts
Round 2: (kfb, k1) 5 times. 15 sts
Round 3: (kfb, k2) 5 times. 20 sts
Round 4: (kfb, k3) 5 times. 25 sts

Round 5: (kfb, k4) 5 times. 30 sts
Rounds 6–7: Knit.
Round 8: (k2tog, k4) 5 times. 25 sts
Rounds 9–10: Knit.
Round 11: (k2tog, k3) 5 times. 20 sts
Rounds 12–23: Knit.
Round 24: K18, k2tog. 19 sts
Round 25: K17, k2tog. 18 sts
Round 26: K16, k2tog. 17 sts
Round 27: K15, k2tog. 16 sts
Round 28: Knit. Bind off. Stuff the leg, filling it more firmly in the foot.

Peg Leg

The peg leg is made in two parts: first, the peg-leg pants, then the peg itself. Once made, join these pieces and stuff the completed peg leg.

Peg-Leg Pants

Using the pants color (gray) yarn, CO 18 stitches, pm, and join to knit in the round.
Rounds 1-3: Knit.
Round 4: Kfb, k17. 19 sts
Round 5: Knit.
Round 6: Kfb, k18. 20 sts
Bind off leaving a tail of 7 inches.

Peg

Using the peg color (tan) yarn, CO 16 stitches, pm, and join to knit in the round.
Round 1: Knit.
Round 2: k2tog, k6, k2tog, k6. 14 sts
Rounds 3–4: Knit.
Round 5: k2tog, k5, k2tog, k5 12 sts
Rounds 6–7: Knit.
Round 8: K2tog, k4, k2tog, k4. 10 sts
Rounds 9–10: Knit.
Round 11: K2tog, k3, k2tog, k3. 8 sts
Rounds 12–13: Knit.
Round 14: K2tog, k2, k2tog, k2. 6 sts
Rounds 15–16: Knit.
Round 17: K2tog, k1, k2tog, k1. 4 sts
Cut the yarn leaving a tail of 7 inches. Pull the tail through remaining 4 stitches. Knot, and pull the knot into inside of the peg leg.

Join the peg to the peg-leg pants: Insert the peg into the peg-leg pants. Use the tail from the bound-off edge of the peg-leg pants to attach the peg. Stuff the entire peg leg firmly.

Assembly

You should now have eight pieces as shown at right:

For each leg, arm, and eye, thread the remaining tail onto a yarn needle, and use a ladder stitch to attach each piece to the body, using the photos as a guide.

Note for the arms: to allow the arms to lay flat against side of body, flatten the top of each arm before sewing as shown below.

Using the separate templates, cut out the felt pieces. Use a blanket stitch to attach all pieces.

Eye Patch
Use black thread. Sew the patch onto the left eye, then use a length of black yarn to create the strap.

Eyes
Use brown thread. Sew the eyeball first, followed by the iris, the pupil, and the eyelid last.

Belt Buckle
Use black thread. Sew on the belt buckle using a blanket stitch from inside to outside all the way around.

Sword Blade
Use brown thread. Put the two 2 pieces of the blade together, and sew all the way around the perimeter.

Sword
Assemble the blade, attach the handle, and make a belt loop to hold the finished sword.

Belt Loop
Use black thread. On the belt, attach the belt loop to hold the sword. Secure the belt loop on each. Insert the sword.

Teeth
Use white thread for the white teeth and dark yellow thread for the gold tooth. Sew the teeth onto the body.

Shiver me timbers! You're finished!

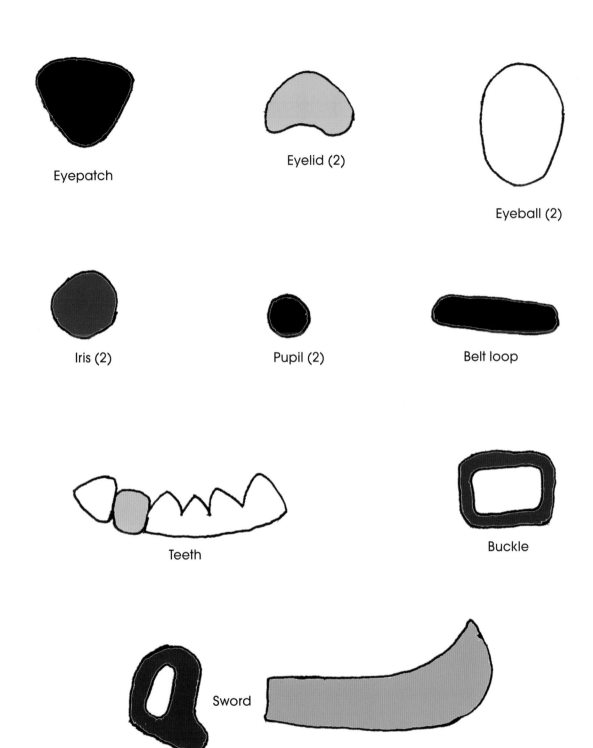

Eyepatch

Eyelid (2)

Eyeball (2)

Iris (2)

Pupil (2)

Belt loop

Teeth

Buckle

Sword

Ninja

My son Drew is constantly begging me to knit something for him. My daughter has an endless collection of handmade toys but I've always found it far more challenging to come up with ideas suitable for a 10-year-old boy. One afternoon while watching Drew practice his ninja moves on his little sister, inspiration hit.

Materials

- 2 skeins (300 yds.) Cascade 220 number 8555 (black) or Cascade 220 number 8895 (red)
- 1 set US 7 (4.5mm) double pointed needles
- Toy stuffing
- 1 piece white felt 3 x 5 in.
- 1 piece black felt 1 x 10 inches plus 1 piece black felt 2 x 2 in.
- 2 pieces gray felt 1 x 1 in.
- Red, gray, black, and white thread

Glossary of abbreviations

CO	cast on
dpn	double pointed needles(s)
k	knit
k2tog	knit two together
kfb	knit into front and back of stitch
p	purl
pm	place marker
ssk	slip slip knit. Increase by knitting into the front and then back of a stitch
st[s]	stitch[es]

Body

knit from the head down.

Using 2 strands of yarn, CO 14, pm, join to knit in the round.

Round 1: K2, kfb, k3, kfb, k2, kfb, k3, kfb. 18 sts

Round 2: K2, kfb, k5, kfb, k2, kfb, k5, kfb. 22 sts

Round 3: K2, kfb, k7, kfb, k2, kfb, k7, kfb. 26 sts

Round 4: K2, kfb, k9, kfb, k2, kfb, k9, kfb. 30 sts

Round 5: K2, kfb, k11, kfb, k2, kfb, k11, kfb 34 sts

Round 6: K2, kfb, k13, kfb, k2, kfb, k13, kfb. 38 sts

Round 7: K2, kfb, k15, kfb, k2, kfb, k15, kfb. 42 sts

Round 8: K2, kfb, k17, kfb, k2, kfb, k17, kfb. 46 sts

Round 9: K2, kfb, k19, kfb, k2, kfb, k19, kfb. 50 sts

Round 10: K2, kfb, k21, kfb, k2, kfb, k21, kfb. 54 sts

Round 11: K2, kfb, k23, kfb, k2, kfb, k23, kfb. 58 sts

Round 12: Knit.

Round 13: K2, kfb, k25, kfb, k2, kfb, k25, kfb. 62 sts

Round 14: Knit.

Round 15: K2, kfb, k27, kfb, k2, kfb, k27, kfb. 66 sts

Round 16: Knit.

Round 17: K2, kfb, k29, kfb, k2, kfb, k29, kfb. 70 sts

Rounds 18-35: Knit.

Round 36: K2, k2tog, k29, ssk, k2, k2tog, k29, ssk. 66 sts

Round 37: Knit.

Row 38: K2, k2tog, k27, ssk, k2, k2tog, k27, ssk. 62 sts

Round 39: Knit.

Round 40: K2, k2tog, k25, ssk, k2, k2tog, k25, ssk. 58 sts

Round 41: Knit.

Round 42: K2, k2tog, k23, ssk, k2, k2tog, k23, ssk. 54 sts

Round 43: K2, k2tog, k21, ssk, k2, k2tog, k21, ssk. 50 sts

Round 44: K2, k2tog, k19, ssk, k2, k2tog, k19, ssk. 46 sts

Round 45: K2, k2tog, k17, ssk, k2, k2tog, k17, ssk. 42 sts

Round 46: K2, k2tog, k15, ssk, k2, k2tog, k15, ssk. 38 sts

Pause and stuff head nearly full.

Round 47: Knit.

Round 48: K2, kfb, k15, kfb, k2, kfb, k15, kfb. 42 sts

Round 49: Knit.

Round 50: K2, kfb, k17, kfb, k2, kfb, k17, kfb. 46 sts

Round 51-57: Knit.

Round 58: K2, k2tog, k17, ssk, k2, k2tog, k17, ssk. 42 sts

Round 59: Knit.

Round 60: K2, k2tog, k15, ssk, k2, k2tog, k15, ssk. 38 sts

Round 61: Knit.

Round 62: K2, k2tog, k13, ssk, k2, k2tog, k13, ssk. 34 sts

Round 63: K2, k2tog, k11, ssk, k2, k2tog, k11, ssk. 30 sts

Round 64: K2, k2tog, k9, ssk, k2, k2tog, k9, ssk. 26 sts

Round 65: K2, k2tog, k7, ssk, k2, k2tog, k7, ssk. 22 sts

Pause and stuff body nearly full.

Round 66: K2, k2tog, k5, ssk, k2, k2tog,

k5, ssk. 18 sts
Round 67: K2, k2tog, k3, ssk, k2, k2tog, k3, ssk. 14 sts
Round 68: K2, k2tog, k1, ssk, k2, k2tog, k1, ssk. 10 sts
Round 69: K2tog 5 times. 5 sts
Cut yarn and pull tail through remaining stitches. Stuff body completely full. Pull stitches tight, knot, and pull knot to inside of toy. Use a piece of yarn and a yarn needle to sew up the hole in the top of the head.

Arms (make 2)
Using 2 strands of yarn, CO 6, pm, join to knit in the round.
Round 1: Kfb, k1, kfb twice, k1, kfb. 10 sts

Round 2: Kfb, k3, kfb twice, k3, kfb. 14 sts
Rounds 3-4: Knit.
Round 5: K2tog, k3, ssk, k2tog, k3, ssk. 10 sts
Rounds 6-9: Knit.
Round 10: Kfb, k3, kfb twice, k3, kfb. 14 sts
Round 11: Knit.
Round 12: Kfb, k5, kfb twice, k5, kfb. 18 sts
Bind off.

Legs (make 2)
Using 2 strands of yarn, CO 6, pm, join to knit in the round.
Round 1: Kfb, k1, kfb twice, k1, kfb. 10 sts

Round 2: Kfb, k3, kfb twice, k3, kfb. 14 sts
Round 3: Kfb, k5, kfb twice, k5, kfb. 18 sts
Rounds 4-6: Knit.
Round 7: K2tog, k5, ssk, k2tog, k5, ssk. 14 sts
Rounds 8-12: Knit.
Round 13: Kfb, k5, kfb twice, k5, kfb. 18 sts
Round 14 : Knit.
Round 15: Kfb, k7, kfb twice, k7, kfb. 22 sts
Round 16: Knit.
Round 17 Kfb, k9, kfb twice, k9, kfb. 26 sts
Bind off.

Assembly

Stuff arms and legs firmly. Beginning with the arms, sew each to side of body using ladder stitch and black yarn. Align legs just under arms. Attach using ladder stitch. Cut all pieces out of felt. Center white felt rectangle on center of head. Attach using red thread and a blanket stitch. Attach eyes with black thread. Wrap black belt diagonally around body. Pin in place, then secure with blanket stitch. Carefully pin ninja stars on belt, and secure with blanket stitch.

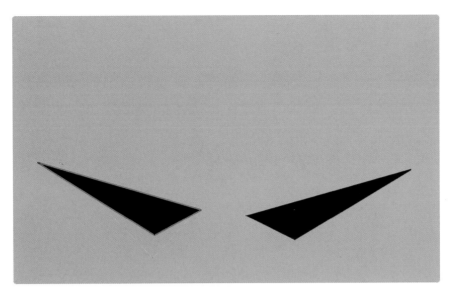

Eyes

Belt

Shuriken

Vampiric Panda

Contrary to popular belief, not all pandas subsist entirely on bamboo. Here deep in the mountain wilderness, we have the little known, but terribly ferocious vampiric panda bear. His new diet may be the result of a lack of bamboo growing in the wild, or perhaps he's learning new habits from the local black bears. Regardless, he may be cute, but lock up your chicken coops. He's always hungry.

Materials

- 1 skein Cascade 220 in 8555 (black)
- 1 skein Cascade 220 in 8505 (white)
- 1 set US 6 (4mm) double pointed needles
- Toy stuffing
- Yarn needle
- Embroidery needle
- Scraps of felt in black, white, and light blue

Glossary of abbreviations

CO	cast on
k	knit
k2tog	knit two together
kfb	knit into front and back of stitch
p	purl
pfb	purl into front and back of stitch
pm	place marker
st[s]	stitch[es]

Head
Using white yarn and US 6 (4mm) needles, CO 6, pm join to knit in the round. Split stitches evenly between 3 needles.
Round 1: Kfb 6 times. 12 sts
Round 2 and all even numbered rounds: Knit.
Round 3: (Kfb, k1) 6 times. 18 sts
Round 5: (Kfb, k2) 6 times. 24 sts
Round 7: (Kfb, k3) 6 times. 30 sts
Round 9: (Kfb, k4) 6 times. 36 sts
Round 11: (Kfb, k5) 6 times. 42 sts
Round 13: (Kfb, k6) 6 times. 48 sts
Rounds 14–22: Knit.
Round 23: (K2tog, k6) 6 times. 42 sts
Round 25: (K2tog, k5) 6 times. 36 sts
Round 27: (K2tog, k4) 6 times. 30 sts
Round 29: (K2tog, k3) 6 times. 24 sts
Round 31: (K2tog, k2) 6 times. 18 sts
Bind off.

Body
Using white yarn and US 6 (4mm) needles, CO 18, pm, join to knit in the round.
Round 1: Knit.
Round 2: (Kfb, k4, kfb twice, k1, kfb) twice. 26 sts
Round 3: Knit.
Round 4: (Kfb, k6, kfb, k5) twice. 30 sts
Round 5: Knit.
Round 6: (Kfb, k8, kfb twice, k3, kfb) twice. 38 sts
Round 7: Knit.
Round 8: (Kfb, k10, kfb, k7) twice. 42 sts
Knit 4 rounds. Switch to black yarn. Knit 8 more rounds.
Round 21: (Kfb, k5) 6 times. 36 sts
Round 22 and all even numbered rounds: Knit.
Round 23: (K2tog, k4) 6 times. 30 sts
Round 25: (K2tog, k3) 6 times. 24 sts
Round 27: (K2tog, k2) 6 times. 18 sts
Round 29: (K2tog, k1) 6 times. 12 sts
Round 31: K2tog 6 times. 6 sts
Break yarn. Pull tail through remaining stitches. Pull tight, knot and pull tail to inside of toy.

Legs (knit 2)
Using white yarn and US 6 (4mm) needles, CO 5, pm join to knit in the round.
Round 1: Kfb 5 times. 10 sts
Round 2: (Kfb, k1) 5 times. 15 sts
Round 3: (Kfb, k2) 5 times. 20 sts
Round 4: Knit.
Switch to black yarn.
Knit 7 rounds. Bind off.

Arms (knit 2)
Using black yarn and US 6 (4mm) needles, CO 5, pm join to knit in the round.
Round 1: Kfb 5 times. 10 sts
Knit 11 rounds. Bind off.

Ears (knit 2)
Using black yarn, and two US 6 (4mm) needles CO 3.
Use stockinette st. as follows:
Row 1: K1, kfb, k1. 4 sts
Row 2: P1, pfb twice, p1. 6 sts
Row 3: Knit.
Row 4: P1, pfb, p2, pfb, p1. 8 sts
Row 5: Knit.
Bind off.

Assembly

Stuff head and body firmly. Center opening on head over body. Use tail from head to seam together using ladder stitch. Stuff legs firmly. Center under boy, and attach using ladder stitch. Stuff arms lightly. Flatten and sew to sides using ladder stitch. Sew ears to top of head, purl-side forward.

Cut pieces from felt. Attach eyes using brown thread and blanket stitch, beginning with the black, followed by the white, blue iris, then pupil. Attach mouth and then teeth in the same manner.

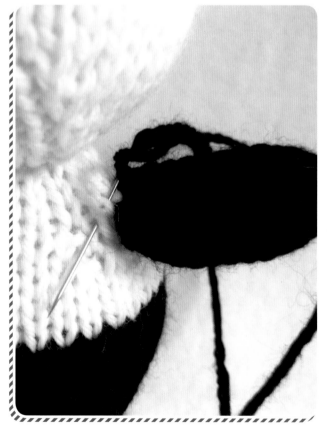

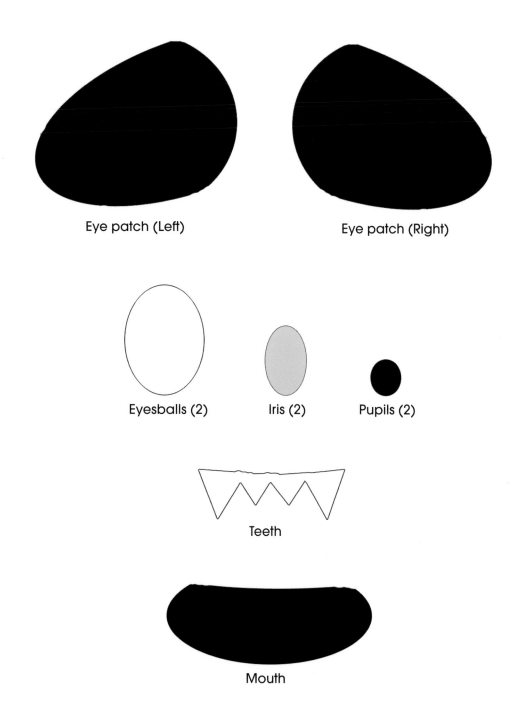

Eye patch (Left)   Eye patch (Right)

Eyesballs (2)   Iris (2)   Pupils (2)

Teeth

Mouth

Oleander

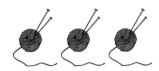

Oleander is the kind of friend you keep if you like standing out in a crowd. It's difficult to ignore a bright red monster with jagged black teeth. But you have to admit, his smile is still charming. Look into his lovely blue eyes for a few seconds, and he'll win your heart, guaranteed. He relishes the attention.

Materials

- 1 skein Cascade 220 in 8895
- 1 skein Cascade 220 in 8010
- Small scraps of felt in dark blue and medium blue
- Toy stuffing
- White and red embroidery floss
- 1 set US 6 (4mm) double pointed needles

Glossary of abbreviations

BO	bind off
CO	cast on
dpn	double pointed needles(s)
k	knit
k2tog	knit two together
kfb	knit into front and back of stitch
p	purl
pm	place marker
st[s]	stitch[es]
St st	stockinette stitch

Body (Knit from the bottom up)
Using US 6 dpn and red yarn, CO 6, pm join to knit in the round. Split stitches evenly between 3 needles.
Round 1: Kfb 6 times. 12 sts
Round 2 and all even numbered rounds: Knit.
Round 3: (Kfb, k1) 6 times. 18 sts
Round 5: (Kfb, k2) 6 times. 24 sts
Round 7: (Kfb, k3) 6 times. 30 sts
Round 9: (Kfb, k4) 6 times. 36 sts
Round 11: (Kfb, k5) 6 times. 42 sts
Round 13: (Kfb, k6) 6 times. 48 sts
Round 15: (Kfb, k7) 6 times. 54 sts
Round 17: (Kfb, k8) 6 times. 60 sts
Round 19: (Kfb, k9) 6 times. 66 sts
Rounds 20–24: Knit.
Round 25: (Ssk, k9) 6 times. 60 sts
Rounds 26–27: Knit.
Round 28: (Ssk, k8) 6 times. 54 sts
Rounds 29–30: Knit.
Continue to decrease 6 sts every third round until 30 sts remain, stuffing the toy as you go.
Knit 3 rounds even.

Begin head
Round 1: (Kfb, k4) 6 times. 36 sts
Turn and begin knitting straight.
Row 2: Purl.

Row 3: (Kfb, k5) 6 times. 42 sts
Row 4: Purl.
Continue to increase 6 sts every other row until you have 54 sts.
Knit 14 rows in stockinette st.
Begin intarsia for face:
Row 19: K20, add white yarn, k14, switch back to red, k20.
Row 20: P20 in red, p14 in white, k20 in red.
Continue 7 more rows in this pattern.
Row 28: Purl all the way across in red.
Row 29–34: Stockinette st in red.
Begin dividing for eye stalks:
BO 9, place next 9 sts on scrap yarn, BO 18, place 9 sts on scrap yarn, BO 9.
Seam up back of head using ladder stitch. Fold head in half, and seam across the top, using ladder stitch to pull bound off stitches together, stuffing head firmly as you go.

Begin eyes
Pick up the 9 sts from right eye on dpn needles, divide evenly, pm, join to knit in the round.
Round 1: (Kfb, k2) 3 times. 12 sts
Round 2: Knit.
Round 3: (Kfb, k1) 6 times. 18 sts
Round 4: Knit.

Round 5: (Kfb, k2) 6 times. 24 sts
Rounds 6–9: Knit.
Switch to white yarn.
Knit 3 rounds.
Switch to red yarn.
Round 13: (Kfb, k3) 6 times. 30 sts
Round 14: Knit.
Round 15: (Kfb, k4) 6 times. 36 sts
Round 16: Knit.
Round 17: (Ssk, k4) 6 times. 30 sts
Round 18: Knit.
Round 19: (Ssk, k3) 6 times. 24 sts
Continue decreasing 6 sts every other round until 6 sts remain. Break yarn, pull tail through remaining sts. Fill eye completely with stuffing. Knot, and pull to inside of toy. Repeat for left eye.

Legs (make 2)
Using red yarn, CO 6, pm, join to knit in the round.
Round 1: Kfb 6 times. 12 sts
Round 2 and all even numbered rounds: Knit.

Round 3: (Kfb, k1) 6 times. 18 sts
Round 5: (Kfb, k2) 6 times. 24 sts
Round 7: (Kfb, k3) 6 times. 30 sts
Round 9: (Kfb, k4) 6 times. 36 sts
Knit 6 rounds even. Bind off.

Right Arm
Using red yarn CO 15, pm, join to knit in the round.
Rounds 1–22: Knit.
Round 23: (Kfb, k2) 5 times. 20 sts
Round 24; Knit.
Round 25: (Kfb, k3) 5 times. 25 sts
Rounds 26–27: Knit.

Switch to white yarn.
Rounds 28–31: Knit.
Switch to red yarn.
Round 32: Knit.
Round 33: (K2tog, k3) 5 times. 20 sts
Round 34: (K2tog, k2) 5 times. 15 sts
Round 35: (K2tog, k1) 5 times. 10 sts
Round 36: K2tog 5 times. 5 sts
Break yarn, pull through remaining sts, knot, and pull to inside of hand.

Left Arm
Repeat rounds 1–25 as for right arm.
Switch to white yarn.

Round 26–27: Knit.
Switch to red yarn.
Rounds 28–29: Knit.
Switch to white yarn.
Rounds 30–31: Knit.
Switch to red yarn.
Round 32: Knit.
Round 33: (K2tog, k3) 5 times. 20 sts
Round 34: (K2tog, k2) 5 times. 15 sts
Round 35: (K2tog, k1) 5 times. 10 sts
Round 36: K2tog 5 times. 5 sts
Break yarn, pull through remaining sts, knot, and pull to inside of hand.

Assembly

Center legs on front of body. Seam using ladder stitch, pausing 2/3 of the way through to stuff. Stuff arms loosely, and attach to sides of body using ladder stitch.

Cut all felt pieces. Using blanket stitch and white thread, attach eyes, medium blue followed by dark blue. Attach teeth using red thread.

Eyeballs (2)

Pupils (2)

Teeth

Ratchet

How could anyone not love robots? They are fascinating on so many imaginative levels. In popular culture, robots are created not only to perform a number of practical tasks, but they also seek to imitate how we as humans interact with the world around us. Personally, I love the very idea of having a robot around to do my housework and laundry, tell me jokes, and bring me beverages while I relax and knit. Of course, I can't promise this robot will do any of those things. He has a singular objective … compulsory cuteness.

Materials

- 1skein Cascade 220 in 2409 (green)
- 1 skein Cascade 220 in 8555 (black)
- 1 skein Cascade 220 in 8400 (gray)
- 1 set US 6 (4mm) double pointed needles
- Toy stuffing
- Yarn needle
- Embroidery needle
- Scraps of felt in black, white, and light green

Glossary of abbreviations

BO	bind off
CO	cast on
k	knit
k2tog	knit two together
kfb	knit into front and back of stitch
pm	place marker
st[s]	stitch[es]

Body

Using green yarn, CO 20.
Complete 8 rows in stockinette.
Row 9: Knit 20, CO 34. 54 sts
Pm, split stitches evenly amongst needles, join to knit in the round.
Knit 28 rounds.
Round 38: K20, BO 34. 20 sts
Row 39: Turn, p20.
Complete 7 more rows in stockinette.
Bind off, leaving a 12 in. tail.

Head

Using green yarn, CO 38, pm, join to knit in the round.
Knit 20 rounds.
Round 21: BO 23, k15. 15 sts
Turn, complete 6 rows in stockinette. Bind off, leaving 12 in. tail.

Feet (make 2)

Using black yarn, CO 8, pm, join to knit in the round.
Round 1: Kfb 8 times. 16 sts
Round 2: (kfb, k2, kfb) 4 times. 24 sts
Knit 6 rounds.

Bind off, leaving 12 in. tail.

Arms (make 2)

Using black yarn, CO 14, pm, join to knit in the round.
Knit 24 rounds.
Divide for claws:
Round 1: K7, place next 7 stitches on scrap yarn. Join the first 7 sts to knit in the round.
Knit 7 rounds.
Break yarn, pull tail through remaining sts. Using tail, weave yarn through inside of claw, pulling to curve claw towards center. Place sts from scrap yarn on needles. Reattach yarn, and begin knitting in the round. Complete the same as for first half of claw.

Antenna (make 2)

Using gray yarn, CO 5, join to knit in the round. Knit an i-cord ¾ in. long. Break yarn, pull tail through remaining stitches.

Assembly

Body

Fold top flap over. Use tail and ladder stitch to sew into place. Stuff body mostly full. Fold bottom flap over and seam the same as for the top, pausing to stuff firmly when nearly complete.

Head

Fold flap over and secure same as for body. Stuff firmly, pressing into rectangular shape. Center head on top of body, secure using ladder stitch.
Feet: Sew to bottom using ladder stitch, pausing to stuff firmly.

Arms

Stuff lightly. Sew to sides of body using ladder stitch.

Antenna

Center on sides of head, attaching using ladder stitch.

Face

Cut all pieces from felt. Sew black rectangle onto face using blanket stitch. Follow with white rectangle. Center eyes on face, and sew into place. Use a single strand of black thread and running stitch to create mouth.

Control panel

Cut pieces from felt. Secure white panel to black. Use three strands of red thread to embroider heart and circuits. Sew buttons onto chest using running stitch.

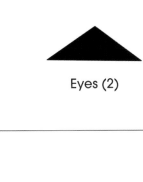

Eyes (2)

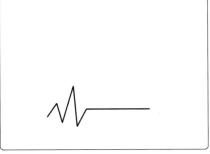

Face - white rectangle

Face - black rectangle

Control panel

Control panel background

Buttons

Buttons background

Alligator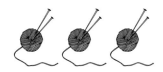

I have been told by some that my work can be rather macabre. While I can understand how someone might come to this conclusion, I would also argue that this particular pattern is meant rather as a cautionary tale. Anyone who has grown up in the southern US, or alligator country, knows there are certain activities you should avoid, such as swimming in an alligator pond, taking your pet alligator for a walk, or kicking your neighbor's pet alligator in the face. You'd think these would be obvious, but some people are surprisingly naïve about these things.

Materials

- 1 skein Cascade 220 in 9430 (dark green)
- 1 skein Cascade 220 in 8914 (pea green)
- 1 skein Cascade 220 in 8010 (off white)
- 1 skein Cascade 220 in 7816 (blue)
- 1 set 6 US (4mm) double pointed needles
- 1 set 5 US (3.75mm) double pointed needles
- Scraps of black and green felt
- Embroidery floss
- Yarn needle
- Embroidery needle
- Toy stuffing
- 2 small buttons

Glossary of abbreviations

BO	bind off
CO	cast on
k	knit
k2tog	knit two together
kfb	knit into front and back of stitch
p	purl
p2tog	purl two together
pfb	purl into front and back of stitch
pm	place marker
ssk	slip slip knit slipped stitches together
st[s]	stitch[es]

Top of head
Using 2 double pointed US 6 (4mm) needles and dark green yarn, CO 8 sts.
Row 1: K1, kfb, k4, kfb, k1. 10 sts
All even rows 2–20 purl.
Row 3: Knit.
Row 5: K2, kfb, k4, kfb, k2. 12 sts
Row 7: Knit.
Row 9: K3, kfb, k4, kfb, k3. 14 sts
Row 11: Knit.
Row 13: K4, kfb, k4, kfb, k4. 16 sts
Row 15: Knit.
Row 17: K5, kfb, k4, kfb, k5. 18 sts
Row 19: Knit.
Row 21: K6, kfb, k4, kfb, k6. 20 sts
Row 22: P7, pfb, p4, pfb, p7. 22 sts
Row 23: K8, kfb, k4, kfb, k8. 24 sts
Row 24: P9, pfb twice, p2, pfb twice, p9. 28 sts
Row 25: K9, k2 tog, ssk, k2, k2tog, ssk, k9. 24 sts
Row 26: P9, p2tog, p4, p2tog, p9. 22 sts
Row 27: K8, k2tog, k4, ssk, k8. 20 sts
Row 28: P7, p2tog, p4, p2tog, p7. 18 sts
Row 29: K6, k2tog, k4, ssk, k6. 16 sts
Leave stitches on needle. Use remaining needles to begin bottom jaw.

Bottom jaw
Using 2 double pointed US 6 (4mm) needles and dark green yarn, CO 6 sts.
Row 1: K1, kfb, k2, kfb, k1. 8 sts
All even rows 2–22 purl.
Row 3: Knit.
Row 5: K1, kfb, k4, kfb, k1. 10 sts
Row 7: Knit.
Row 9: K2, kfb, k4, kfb, k2. 12 sts
Row 11: Knit.
Row 13: K3, kfb, k4, kfb, k3. 14 sts
Row 15: Knit.
Row 17: K4, kfb, k4, kfb, k4. 16 sts
Row 19: Knit
Row 21: K5, kfb, k4, kfb, k5. 18 sts

With wrong sides held together, join jaws and begin body:
Row 1: Knit across stitches on the bottom jaw, then across the stitches from the top jaw.
Join to knit in the round. 34 sts
Round 2: Knit.
Round 3: K2, kfb, k12, kfb, k4, kfb, k10, kfb, k2. 38 sts
Round 4: Knit.
Round 5: K2, kfb, k14, kfb, k4, kfb, k12, kfb, k2. 42 sts
Round 6: Knit.
Round 7: K2, k2tog, k14, ssk, k4, k2tog, k12, ssk, k2. 38 sts
Round 8: K2, k2tog, k12, ssk, k4, k2tog, k10, ssk, k2. 34 sts
Round 9: K2, k2tog, k10, ssk, k4, k2tog, k8, ssk, k2. 30 sts
Round 10: K2, k2tog, k8, ssk, k2tog, k6,

ssk, k2. 26 sts
Round 11: Knit.
Round 12: K2, kfb, k8, kfb, k4, kfb, k6, kfb, k2. 30 sts
Round 13: K2, kfb, k10, kfb, k4, kfb, k8, kfb, k2. 34 sts
Round 14: K2, kfb, k12, kfb, k4, kfb, k10, kfb, k2. 38 sts
Round 15: K2, kfb, k14, kfb, k4, kfb, k12, kfb, k2. 42 sts
Round 16: K2, kfb, k16, kfb, k4, kfb, k6, kfb, place marker, kfb, k6, kfb, k2. 48 sts
Round 17: Knit.
Round 18: K2, kfb, k18, kfb, k4, kfb, k18, kfb, k2. 52 sts
Round 19: Knit.
Round 20: K2, kfb, k20, kfb, k4, kfb, k20, kfb, k2. 56 sts
Round 21: Knit.
Round 22: K40, kfb on each side of marker, k12. 58 sts
Continue to increase one stitch on each side of the marker every third round 2 more times. 62 sts
Knit 2 rounds even.
On the next round, knit to 2 stitches before marker, k2tog, ssk, knit to end. 60 sts
Continue to decrease 1 stitch on each side of the marker every third round 2 times. 56 sts

Begin tail
Round 1: K2, k2tog, k20, ssk, k4, k2tog, k20, ssk, k2 . 52 sts
Round 2: K2, k2tog, k18, ssk, k4, k2tog, k18, ssk, k2. 48 sts
Round 3: K2, k2tog, k16, ssk, k4, k2tog, k16, ssk, k2. 44 sts
Round 4: K2, k2tog, k14, ssk, k4, k2tog, k14, ssk, k2. 40 sts
Round 5: K2, k2tog, k12, ssk, k4, k2tog, k12, ssk, k2. 36 sts
Round 6: K2, k2tog, k10, ssk, k4, k2tog, k10, ssk, k2. 32 sts
Round 7: K2, k2tog, k8, ssk, k4, k2tog, k8, ssk, k2. 28 sts
Round 8: K2, k2tog, k6, ssk, k4, k2tog,

k6, ssk, k2. 24 sts
Round 9: Knit to 2 stitches before marker k2tog, ssk, knit to end. Continue to decrease a stitch on each side of the marker every 10th round, until there are 12 sts remaining.
Next round: (K2tog, k1) 4 times. 8 sts
Next round: K2tog 4 times. 4 sts
Pull yarn through remaining stitches to draw hole closed. Knot and pull knot to inside of tail using a yarn needle.

Inside of mouth bottom
Using pea green yarn and 2 double pointed US 6 (4mm) needles, CO 6 sts.
Row 1: Knit.
Row 2: and all even rows Purl.
Row 3: Kfb, k4, kfb. 8 sts
Row 5: Knit.
Row 7: Kfb, k6, kfb. 10 sts
Continue to increase on each end of every fourth row until you have 16 sts.
Complete 3 more rows in stockinette.
Bind off.

Inside of mouth top
Using pea green yarn and 2 double pointed US 6 (4mm) needles, CO 8 sts.
Row 1: Knit.
Row 2: and all even rows Purl.
Row 3: Kfb, k6, kfb. 10 sts
Continue to increase on each end of every fourth row until you have 18 sts.
Knit 10 more rows. Bind off.

Spine
Using pea green yarn and 2 double pointed US 6 (4mm) needles, CO 2 sts.
Row 1: Knit
Row 2: Kfb, k1. 3 sts
Row 3: K2, kfb 4 sts
Row 4: Kfb, k3. 5 sts
Row 5: Knit
Row 6: Ssk, k3. 4 sts
Row 7: K2, k2tog 3 sts
Row 8: Ssk, k1. 2 sts
Repeat all 8 rows 15 times.
BO 2 sts.

Legs (make 4)
Using dark green yarn and US 6 (4mm) needles, CO 6 sts. Join to knit in the round.
Round 1: Kfb 6 times. 12 sts
Round 2: (Kfb, k1) 6 times. 18 sts
Round 3: (Kfb, k2) 6 times. 24 sts
Rounds 4–6: Knit.
Round 7: (K2tog, k2) 6 times. 18 sts
Rounds 8–10: Knit.
Round 11: (K2tog, k1) 6 times. 12 sts
Rounds 12–14: Knit.
Bind off.

Teeth (make 2)
Using white yarn and US 5 (3.75mm) needles, CO 5 sts, pm, join to knit in the round.
Round 1: Kfb 5 times. 10 sts
Round 2: (Kfb, k1) 5 times. 15 sts
Round 3: Knit.
Bind off.

Lady legs (make 2)
Using white yarn and US 6 (4mm) needles, CO 18 sts, pm , join to knit in the round.
Knit 15 rounds.
Round 16: (K2tog, k1) 6 times. 12 sts
Round 17: K2tog 6 times. 6 sts
Break yarn, knot pull to inside of foot.

Shoes (make 2)
Using blue yarn and US 6 (4mm) needles, CO 5 sts, pm, join to knit in the round.
Round 1: Kfb 5 times. 10 sts
Round 2: (Kfb, k1) 5 times. 15 sts
Round 3: (Kfb, k2) 5 times. 20 sts
Rounds 4–5: Knit.
Round 6: BO 8, k12. 12 sts
Turn work, begin knitting straight.
Complete 3 rows in stockinette. Bind off, leaving 6 in. tail.

Assembly

Lightly press all pieces. Place insides of mouth together, right sides touching. Sew together along inside edge using running stitch.

Sew inside of mouth to head with ladder stitch, starting with the top. Pause before seaming lower jaw, to stuff body and top of head. You may have to poke and squeeze toy to fill corners, and make the body plump and round. Finish seaming jaw, stuffing the bottom jaw just before the last few stitches.

Sew spine along center of back. Stuff alligator legs and attach along lower side of body. Sew teeth to upper edge of mouth. Lightly stuff the human legs, flatten edge, and sew to inside edge of mouth. Slide shoes over feet. Use tail to pull across top of foot for the strap. Sew a little button to side of both shoes. Cut felt pieces using template. Use blanket stitch to attach eyes to head, and bottoms of feet.

Eyes (2)

Feet (4)

THIS IS GOING TO GO RIGHT TO MY HIPS

Papaya

I've often wished I had four arms. Think of all the knitting I could accomplish. Granted, I find I can barely multitask with the two I currently have, but still. This monster is lucky enough to have multiple appendages. However, having such short arms can make life a little more difficult. He can't even stretch his hand to scratch hard-to-reach places, much less shovel food into his own mouth. Fortunately, he has big teeth to make up for the shortcoming.

Materials

- 1 skein Cascade 220 in 7803
- 3 yards of white worsted weight yarn
- 1 set US 6 (4mm) double pointed needles
- Scraps of felt in black and white
- Yarn needle
- Embroidery needle
- Thread in white and black
- Toy stuffing

Glossary of abbreviations

BO	bind off
CO	cast on
k	knit
k2tog	knit two together
kfb	knit into front and back of stitch
p	purl
pm	place marker
st[s]	stitch[es]

Body

Using green yarn, CO 20.
Complete 8 rows in stockinette.
Round 9: Knit 20, CO 34. 54 sts
Pm, split stitches evenly amongst needles, join to knit in the round.
Knit 20 rounds.
Round 21: K20, BO 34. 20 sts
Row 22: Turn, p20.
Complete 7 more rows in stockinette.
Bind off, leaving a 12 in. tail.

Legs (knit 2)

CO 8, pm, join to knit in the round.
Round 1: (Kfb, k1) 4 times. 12 sts
Round 2: (Kfb, k1, kfb) 4 times. 20 sts
Round 3: (Kfb, k3, kfb) 4 times. 28 sts
Knit 8 rounds even. Bind off.

Arms (knit 4)

CO 5, pm, join to knit in the round.
Round 1: Kfb 5 times. 10 sts
Round 2: (Kfb, k1) 5 times. 15 sts
Knit 6 rounds. Bind off.

Horns (knit 2)

Using white yarn, CO 10, pm, join to knit in the round.
Rounds 1–2: Knit.
Round 3: (K2, k2tog, k1) twice. 8 sts
Rounds 4–5: Knit.
Round 6: (K1, k2tog, k1) twice. 6 sts
Round 7: Knit.
Break yarn, pull tail through remaining stitches. Weave tail in and out down side of horn and pull to create slight curve. Knot, weave into inside of horn.

Assembly

Body

Fold flap over. Seam using ladder stitch, being careful to keep corners even. Stuff body full. Press flat into shape. Fold over second flap and seam the same way. Stuff legs firmly. Place on bottom of body at edges. Seam into place using ladder stitch. Stuff arms lightly and sew to sides of body. Center horns on top corners of the head. There is no need to stuff horns. Seam into place.

Cut felt pieces from templates. Sew mouth on face using white thread and blanket stitch. Use contrasting thread and running, follow template to create teeth. Sew eyes into place using dark thread.

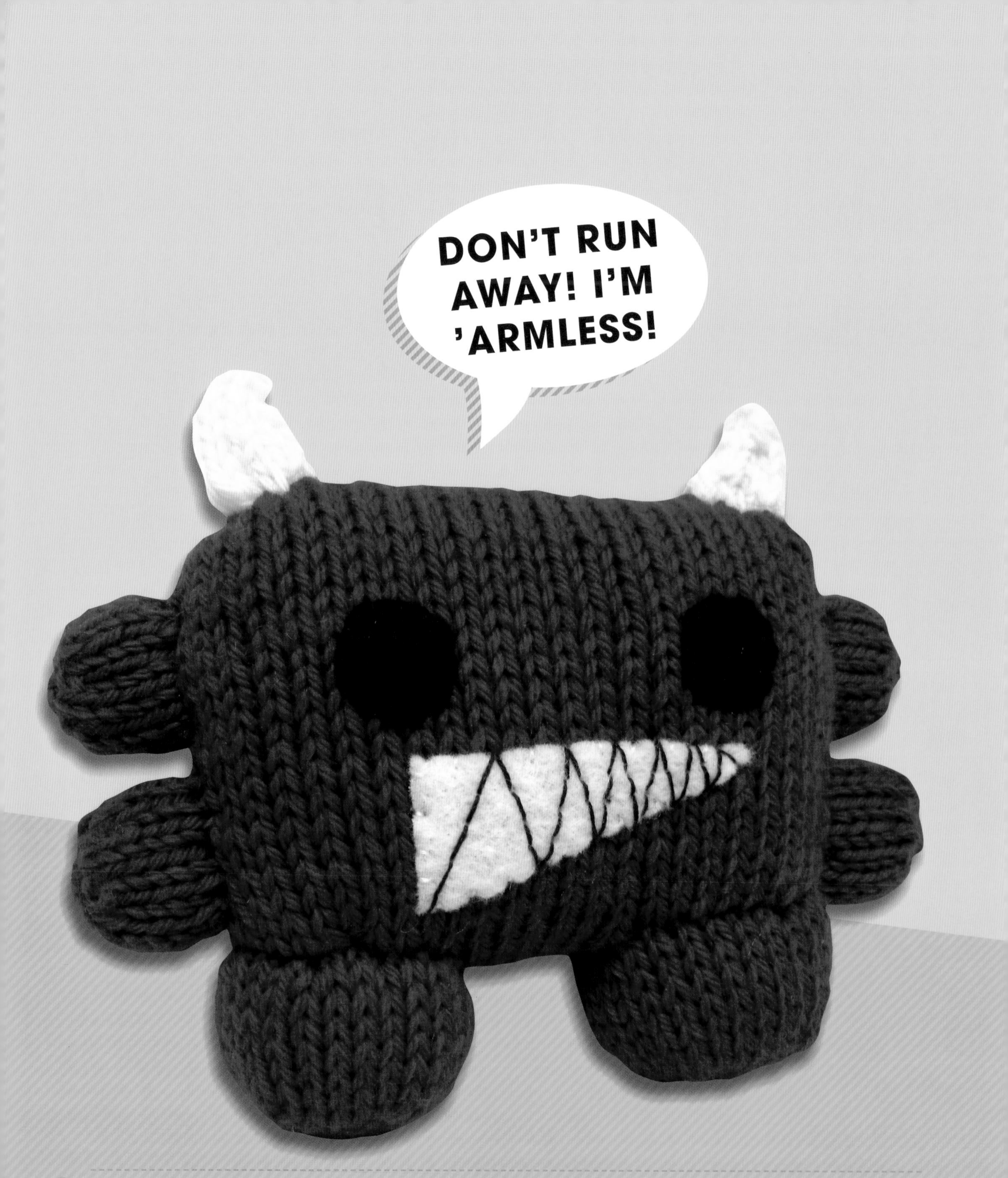
DON'T RUN AWAY! I'M 'ARMLESS!

Eyes (2)

Teeth

Digit

Digit may look relatively harmless, but don't let that fool you into thinking you can launch a sneak attack. Digit not only has eyes on the back of his head, he also has eyes all the way around his head. He's alert and attentive. Nothing gets past him.

Materials

- 1 skein Cascade 220 in 9461
- 1 set US 7 (4.5) double pointed needles
- Scraps of wool felt in white, black, light green, and light blue
- Toy stuffing
- Yarn needle
- Embroidery needle
- Thread

Glossary of abbreviations

CO	cast on
k	knit
k2tog	knit two together
kfb	knit into front and back of stitch
pm	place marker
st[s]	stitch[es]

Body

CO 5, pm, join to knit in the round.
Round 1: Kfb 5 times. 10 sts
Round 2: (Kfb, k1) 5 times. 15 sts
Round 3: (Kfb, k2) 5 times. 20 sts
Round 4: (Kfb, k3) 5 times. 25 sts
Round 5: (Kfb, k4) 5 times. 30 sts
Round 6: (Kfb, k5) 5 times. 35 sts
Round 7: (Kfb, k6) 5 times. 40 sts
Round 8: (Kfb, k7) 5 times. 45 sts
Round 9: (Kfb, k8) 5 times. 50 sts
Rounds 10–16: Knit.
Round 17: (K2tog, k8) 5 times. 45 sts
Rounds 18–21: Knit.
Round 22: (K2tog, k7) 5 times. 40 sts
Rounds 23–26: Knit.
Round 27: (K2tog, k6) 5 times. 35 sts
Rounds 28–34: Knit.
Round 35: (K2tog, k5) 5 times. 30 sts
Split stitches for eyes
Place first 6 sts on a piece of scrap yarn. Repeat around base until stitches are split into 5 eyes.

First eye

Using a double pointed needle, pick up and knit first 6 sts from scrap yarn, CO 12 sts, pm, join to knit in the round. 18 sts
Knit 6 rounds even.

Next round: (Kfb, k4, kfb) 3 times. 24 sts
Next round: Knit.
Next round: (Kfb, k6, kfb) 3 times. 30 sts
Knit 3 rounds even.
Next round: (K2tog, k3) 6 times. 24 sts
Next round: Knit.
Next round (K2tog, k2) 6 times. 18 sts
Next round: Knit.
Next round: (K2tog, k1) 6 times. 12 sts
Next round: K2tog 6 times. 6 sts
Break yarn, knot, pull tail to inside of toy. Stuff eye firmly.

Next eye

Move to the left of the first completed eye. Using a double pointed needle, pick up and knit 6 sts from scrap yarn, CO 6, pick up and knit 6 sts from the base of the inside of the first eye, pm, join to knit in the round.
Continue to work same as for first eye. Complete two more eyes in the same fashion.

Before completing last eye, stuff body firmly.

Last eye

Using a double pointed needle, pick up and knit 6 remaining sts from scrap yarn, pick up and knit 6 sts from base of eye to the left, pick up and knit 6 sts of base of eye to the right, pm, join to knit in the round. Complete eye the same as first four eyes. Pause before closing to stuff last eye.

Use the opening in the center to add additional stuffing. Use a yarn needle to weave through stitches at base and close up the hole, knot, pull tail to inside of toy.

Legs (make 2)

CO 5, pm join to knit in the round.
Round 1: Kfb 5 times. 10 sts
Round 2: (Kfb, k1) 5 times. 15 sts
Round 3: (Kfb, k2) 5 times. 20 sts
Knit 7 rounds. Bind off.

Arms (make 2)

CO 5, pm, join to knit in the round.
Round 1: Kfb 5 times. 10 sts
Round 2: (Kfb, k1) 5 times. 15 sts
Rounds 4–6: Knit.
Round 8: (K2tog, k1) 5 times. 10 sts
Knit 12 rounds.
Bind off, leaving 8 in. tail.

Assembly

Stuff legs firmly. Center under body, and attach using ladder stitch.

Stuff arms lightly. Flatten and sew to sides using ladder stitch.

Cut pieces of felt using template. Center belly on body of toy. Attach using dark green thread and ladder stitch.

Center eyes on head. Attach, beginning with white, followed by green, then black, and finally the eyelid, using a blanket stitch.

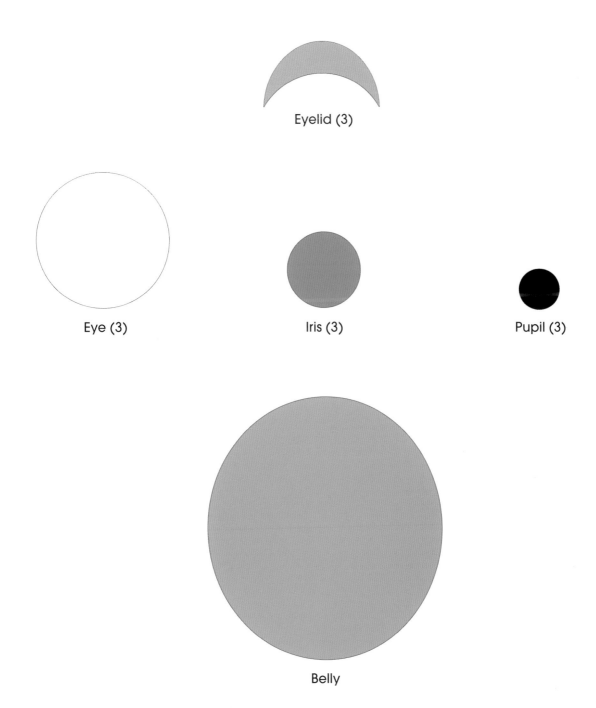

Eyelid (3)

Eye (3)

Iris (3)

Pupil (3)

Belly

Squid

I have a tendency to go a little overboard with Halloween. A few years ago, I created my own robot costume, and won a costume dance-off. The victory of that moment resulted in the need to out-do myself each year. This past year I went as a giant red squid. The costume was enormous, and yes, once again, I won the costume dance-off. What surprised me the most, though, was how much everyone seemed to love the squid. I've never gotten so many hugs. I was rather sad the next day to return to normal human status. So I decided to create a smaller toy version of that costume to commemorate the occasion.

Materials

- 1 skein Cascade 220 in 9488
- 1 set US 6 (4mm) double pointed needles
- Scraps of felt in white, red, and black
- Yarn needle
- Embroidery needle
- Thread
- Toy stuffing

Glossary of abbreviations

BO	bind off
CO	cast on
k	knit
k2tog	knit two together
kfb	knit into front and back of stitch
p	purl
p2tog	purl two together
pm	place marker
ssk	slip, slip, knit slipped stitches together
st[s]	stitch[es]

Body

Using US 6 (4mm) double pointed needles CO 6, pm, join to knit in the round.
Round 1: Kfb 6 times. 12 sts
Rounds 2–3: Knit.
Round 4: (Kfb, k1) 6 times. 18 sts
Rounds 5–6: Knit.
Round 7: (Kfb, k2) 6 times. 24 sts
Continue increasing 6 sts every third round until you have 48 sts.
Knit 7 rounds even.
Round 37: (K2tog, k6) 6 times. 42 sts
Rounds 38–41: Knit.

Legs

Split stitches for legs. Place first 7 stitches on a piece of scrap yarn. Repeat around base until stitches are split into 6 legs.

First leg

Using a double pointed needle, pick up and knit first 7 stitches from scrap yarn, CO 14 stitches, pm, join to knit in the round. 21 sts
Knit 8 rounds even.

Next round: (K2tog, k5) 3 times. 18 sts
Knit 8 rounds even.
Next round: (K2tog, k4) 3 times. 15 sts
Knit 8 rounds even.
Next round: (Kfb, k3) 3 times. 12 sts
Knit 8 rounds even.
Next round: K2tog 6 times. 6 sts
Break yarn, knot, pull tail to inside of toy.
Stuff leg slightly firm.

Next leg

Move to the left of the first completed leg. Using a double pointed needle, pick up and knit 7 sts from scrap yarn, CO 7, pick up and knit 7 sts from the base of the inside of the first leg, pm, join to knit in the round.
Continue to work same as for first leg.
Complete 3 more legs in the same fashion.

Before completing last leg, stuff head and body firmly.

Last leg

Using a double pointed needle, pick up and knit 7 remaining stitches from scrap yarn, pick up and knit 7 stitches from base of leg to the left, pick up and knit 7 stitches of base of leg to the right, pm, join to knit in the round. Complete leg same as first 5 legs. Pause before closing foot to stuff last leg.
Use the opening in the center to add additional stuffing. Use a yarn needle to weave through stitches at base and close up the hole, knot, pull tail to inside of toy.

Tiny fins (make 2)

Using US 6 (4mm) needles CO 9.
Row 1: K1, k2tog, k6. 8 sts
Row 2: P1, p2tog, p5. 7 sts
Continue in stockinette st. decreasing the second st in each row until 3 sts remain.
Break yarn, pull tail through remaining sts, and weave into purl side of fin.

Tentacles (make 2)

Using US 6 (4mm) needles CO 2.
Being knitting an i-cord until it is 8 in.
long. To have varying tentacles, knit the
second 9 in. long.

Next row: Kfb twice. 4 sts. Begin knitting
straight.

Next row: Knit.

Next row: K1, kfb twice, k1. 6 sts

Knit 4 rows in garter st.

Next row: K1, k2tog, ssk, k1. 4 sts

Next row: Knit.

Next row: K2tog, ssk. 2 sts.

Break yarn, pull tail through remaining sts,
weave into back of tentacle.

Assembly
- - - - - - - - - -

Fins
Attach fins to sides of head, knit side
facing forward, using tail and ladder st.

Tentacles
Use tail from cast on edge to sew into
center between legs.

Eyes
Cut eyes from felt using template. Use
blanket stitch and contrasting thread to
sew to face, beginning with the white,
followed by brows, irises, and pupils. Use
a small amount of white thread to create
flecks in eyes.

Eye (2)

Iris (2)

Pupil (2)

Frock

Like so many little girls, Frock simply loves pretty clothes and shoes. Unfortunately, purchasing fancy footwear for someone with six legs can get very expensive. Poor Frock often has to make do with mismatched hand-me-downs from assorted cousins and siblings. Even worse, she is forever loosing her shoes, and driving her mother nearly to tears, tearing apart the house searching for them every morning, trying not to miss the bus.

Materials

- 1 skein Cascade 220 in 9463 (yellow)
- 1 skein Cascade 220 in 8555 (black)
- 1 skein Cascade 220 in 8505 (white)
- 1 set US 6 (4mm) double pointed needles
- Yarn needle
- Toy stuffing
- Embroidery needle
- 2 small black buttons
- 12 small white buttons
- Pieces of felt in black, white, blue, and red
- Black and white embroidery floss

Glossary of abbreviations

BO	bind off
CO	cast on
dpn	double pointed needles[s]
k	knit
k2tog	knit two together
kfb	knit into front and back of stitch
p	purl
p2tog	purl two together
pm	place marker
st[s]	stitch[es]

Body (Knit from the head down)

Using yellow yarn, CO 6, pm, join to knit in the round. Split stitches evenly between 3 needles.

Round 1: Kfb 6 times. 12 sts
Round 2 and all even numbered rounds: Knit.
Round 3: (Kfb, k1) 6 times. 18 sts
Round 5: (Kfb, k2) 6 times. 24 sts
Round 7: (Kfb, k3) 6 times. 30 sts
Round 9: (Kfb, k4) 6 times. 36 sts
Round 11: (Kfb, k5) 6 times. 42 sts
Round 13: (Kfb, k6) 6 times. 48 sts
Round 15: (Kfb, k7) 6 times. 54 sts
Rounds 16–25: Knit.
Round 26: (K2tog, k7) 6 times. 48 sts
Round 27 and all odd numbered rounds: Knit.
Round 28: (K2tog, k6) 6 times. 42 sts
Round 30: (K2tog, k5) 6 times. 36 sts
Round 32: (K2tog, k4) 6 times. 30 sts
Round 34: (K2tog, k3) 6 times. 24 sts
Rounds 35–36: Knit.
Round 37: (K6, kfb, k4, kfb) twice. 28 sts

Round 38 and all even numbered rounds: Knit.
Round 39: (K6, kfb, k6, kfb) twice. 32 sts
Round 41: (K6, kfb, k8, kfb) twice. 36 sts
Round 43: (K6, kfb, k10, kfb) twice. 40 sts
Round 45: (K6, kfb, k12, kfb) twice. 44 sts
Round 47: (K6, kfb, k14, kfb) twice. 48 sts
Knit 15 rounds even.

Legs

Split stitches for legs. Place first 8 stitches on a piece of scrap yarn. Repeat around base until stitches are split into 6 legs.

First leg

Using a dpn needle, pick up and knit first 8 stitches from scrap yarn, CO 16, pm, join to knit in the round. 24 sts
Knit 38 rounds even.
Round 39: (Kfb, k7) 3 times. 27 sts

Knit 6 rounds even.
Round 46: (K2tog, k7) 3 times. 24 sts
Round 47: (K2tog, k2) 6 times. 18 sts
Round 48: (K2tog, k1) 6 times. 12 sts
Round 49: K2tog 6 times. 6 sts
Break yarn, knot, pull tail to inside of toy.
Stuff leg: firmly in the foot, and lightly in the leg.

Next leg

Move to the left of the first completed leg. Using a dpn needle, pick up and knit 8 sts from scrap yarn, CO 8, pick up and knit 8 sts from the base of the inside of the first leg, pm, join to knit in the round. Continue to work same as for first leg. Complete 3 more legs in the same fashion.

Before completing the last leg, stuff head and body firmly.

Last leg

Using a dpn needle, pick up and knit 8 remaining stitches from scrap yarn, pick up and knit 8 stitches from base of leg to the left, pick up and knit 8 stitches of base of leg to the right, pm, join to knit in the round. Complete leg same as first 5 legs. Pause before closing foot to stuff last leg.

Use the opening in the center to add additional stuffing. Use a yarn needle to weave through stitches at base and close up the hole, knot, pull tail to inside of toy.

Arms (make 2)

Using yellow yarn, CO 5, pm, join to knit in the round.
Round 1: Kfb 5 times. 10 sts
Round 2: (Kfb, k1) 5 times. 15 sts
Round 3: (Kfb, k2) 5 times. 20 sts
Rounds 4–7: Knit.
Round 8: (K2tog, k2) 5 times. 15 sts
Knit 18 rounds. Bind off, leaving 8 in. tail.

Dress

Using white yarn, CO 52, pm, join to knit in the round.
Knit 18 rounds even.

Split for front and back of dress:
Round 19: (BO 2, k24) twice. 48 sts

Begin back of dress

Row 20: Turn, p1, p2tog, p18, p2tog, p1. 22 sts
Row 21: K1, k2tog, k16, k2tog, k1. 20 sts
Row 22: P1, p2tog, p14, p2tog, p1. 18 sts
Continue decreasing in this manner until 12 sts remain. Bind off, leaving a 6 in. tail. Connect yarn to remaining stitches, and repeat from row 20 as for back of dress. Slip dress over doll. Pull tails over shoulder and through the opposing corner to make straps. Knot, and weave tail into dress. Sew buttons to front.

Hair

Using black yarn, CO 6, pm, join to knit in the round.
Round 1: Kfb 6 times. 12 sts
Round 2: (Kfb, k1) 6 times. 18 sts
Round 3: (Kfb, k2) 6 times. 24 sts
Round 4: (Kfb, k3) 6 times. 30 sts
Round 5: (Kfb, k4) 6 times. 36 sts
Round 6: (Kfb, k5) 6 times. 42 sts
Round 7: (Kfb, k6) 6 times. 48 sts

Round 8: (Kfb, k7) 6 times. 54 sts
Round 9: BO 14, k40. 40 sts
Row 10: Turn, p40.
Complete 18 rows in stockinette st. Bind off.

Shoes (make 6)

Using black yarn, CO 5, pm, join to knit in the round.
Round 1: Kfb 5 times. 10 sts
Round 2: (Kfb, k1) 5 times. 15 sts
Round 3: (Kfb, k2) 5 times. 20 sts
Round 4: (Kfb, k3) 5 times. 25 sts
Rounds 5–7: Knit.
Round 8: BO 10, knit to end. 15 sts
Row 9: Turn, p13.
Row 10: Knit.
Row 11: Purl.
Bind off, leaving a 6 in. tail.

Assembly

Hair

Center hair on head. Use black yarn to stitch center of hair to center of head. Use straight stitch to sew hair around face, beginning 1/4 in. down sides, across bangs, and 1/4 in. around other side. Leave the bottom edge of hair loose. Weave in loose ends.

Shoes

Pull shoe over feet tightly. Use long tail for strap. Pull across top of foot and secure with knot on other side. Sew small button on outsides.

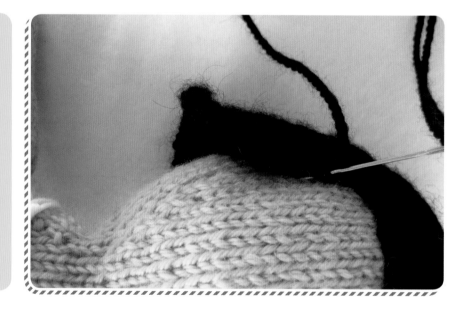

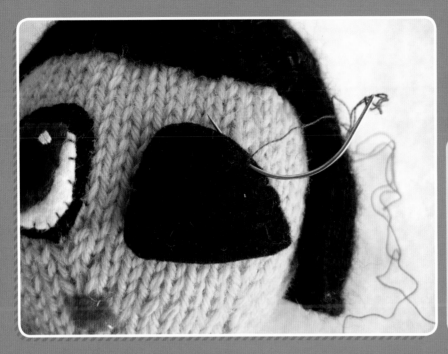

Arms
Stuff lightly and sew to sides of body using ladder stitch.

Felt
Cut all pieces of felt using templates. Use a blanket stitch to attach star to dress, and mouth to face. To attach eyes, beginning with black, followed by white, blue, then pupils. Use 3 strands of white embroidery floss to create flecks in eyes.

Star

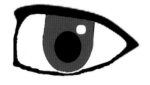

Left eye   Right eye

Mouth

I'M A GREAT DANCER, DESPITE HAVING SIX LEFT FEET!

Gauge, and Finished Toy Size

 = Beginner   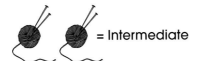 = Intermediate   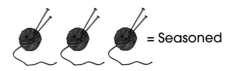 = Seasoned

Owls
Small:
Gauge: 20 sts and 28 rows over 4 in. in stockinette st
Finished toy size: 4 in. tall.
Large:
Gauge: 18 sts and 24 rows over 4 in. in stockinette st
Finished toy size: 6 in. tall.

Frank
Gauge: 20 sts and 28 rows over 4 in. in stockinette st
Finished toy size: 4½ in. tall.

Otto
Gauge: 20 sts and 28 rows over 4 in. in stockinette st
Finished toy size: 13 in. tall.

Flop
Gauge: 14 sts and 18 rows over 4 in. in stockinette st
Finished toy size: 11 in. tall.

Dave
Gauge: 20 sts and 28 rows over 4 in. in stockinette st
Finished toy size: 7 in. tall.

Bo Peeps
Gauge: 16 sts and 22 rows over 4 in. in stockinette st
Finished size: 13 inches

Rosie
Gauge: 20 sts and 24 rows over 4 in. in stockinette st.
Finished toy size: 7 in. tall.

Cyclops
Gauge: 20 sts and 28 rows over 4 in. in stockinette st
Finished toy size: 13 in. tall.

Jacques Crusteau
Gauge: 20 sts and 28 rows over 4 in. in stockinette st
Finished toy size: 13 in. tall.

Mr. Abominable
Gauge: 20 sts and 28 rows over 4 in. in stockinette st
Finished toy size: 9 in. tall.

Peg
Gauge: 20 sts and 28 rows over 4 in. in stockinette st
Finished toy size: 11 in. tall.

Ninja
Gauge: 14 sts and 24 rows over 4 in.
Finshed size: 10 in. tall.

Vampiric Panda
Gauge: 20 sts and 28 rows over 4 in. in stockinette st
Finished toy size: 8½ in. tall.

Oleander
Gauge: 20 sts and 28 rows over 4 in. in stockinette st
Finished toy size: 11 in. tall.

Ratchet
Gauge: 20 sts and 28 rows over 4 in. in stockinette st
Finished toy size: 8 in. tall.

Alligator
Gauge: 20 sts and 28 rows over 4 in. in stockinette st
Finished toy size: 15 in. long.

Papaya
Gauge: 20 sts and 28 rows over 4 in. in stockinette st
Finished toy size: 5 in. tall.

Digit
Gauge: 20 sts and 24 rows over 4 in. in stockinette st.
Finished toy size: 8 in. tall.

Squid
Gauge: 20 sts and 28 rows over 4 in. in stockinette st
Finished toy size: 14 in. tall.

Frock
Gauge: 20 sts and 28 rows over 4 in. in stockinette st
Finished toy size: 16 in. tall.

Cascade is a manufacturer and international distributor of fine yarns, their products are available worldwide. I thank them for supplying all the yarns used in this book.

In the late 1980's, Bob and Jean Dunbabin founded Cascade Yarns in Seattle, Washington with the goal to provide affordable, high-quality yarns. The search for a soft, long-stapled wool brought Bob Dunbabin to Peru, where he found plentiful, light-colored, high lofting wool from sheep (a hybrid of the native Corriedale and Merino) that were raised by Peruvian natives in the Sierra Mountains above 12,000 feet. Largely by word-of-mouth, Cascade 220 became renowned as the affordable high-quality knitting yarn with great yardage that is available in more than 350 Solids, Heathers, Quatros, Tweeds, and Hand Paints. Cascade Yarn is available in a variety of locations in Europe, the UK, Australia and New Zealand.